CHRISTIAN COUNSELING

Pastor James Justin

Dr. Lauretta Justin

Copyright © 2016 by James Justin & Lauretta Justin

Christian Counseling

Course Manual Edition

By James Justin & Lauretta Justin

ISBN-10: 0-9971126-1-1
ISBN-13: 978-0-9971126-1-0

Printed in the United Stated of America.

All rights reserved. No part of this publication may be reproduced, distributed, stored in a retrieval system or transmitted in any form or by any means, electronic, mechanical, photocopying, recording, scanning or otherwise without the prior written permission by the author.

Unless otherwise specified, Biblical quotations are taken from the New King James Version. Copyright © 1982 by Thomas Nelson, Inc.

This publication is designed to provide general information regarding the subject matter addressed. It is sold with the understanding that the author and the publisher are not engaged in rendering legal services. Laws and practices often vary from state to state and from country to country; and if legal and/or professional services are required, they should be sought. The author and the publisher specifically disclaim any liability that is incurred from the use and application of the contents in this publication.

Book Industry Standards and Communications (BISAC) Categories: Bible Studies, Theology, Counseling, Psychology

Keywords: Bible, Christian Counseling, Theology, Counseling, Psychology

CoachJamesJustin.com
6601 Old Winter Garden Rd. Suite 104
Orlando, FL 32835

Products by the Authors

- Christian Counseling by James Justin and Dr. Lauretta Justin

- The Power of Prayer by James Justin and Dr. Lauretta Justin

- 12 Tips to Achieve your Financial Freedom: The Simple Guide to Successfully Manage your Personal Finance by James Justin

- 7 Steps to Develop Healthy Relationships with Anyone by James Justin

- Positive Parenting: 12 Tips to prepare your kids for success by James Justin

- Parenting Digital Natives: What Parents Can Do About The Dangers of Social Media by Dr. Lauretta Justin

- Mindset: How to transform your life from ordinary to extraordinary by James Justin

- CEO OF YOU: How to Create the Business and the Life of Your Dreams by Dr. Lauretta Justin

- 7 Reasons Why We Don't Pursue Our Dreams: How You Can Overcome Them To Get The Life of Your Dreams by Dr. Lauretta Justin

- The Spirit of Christmas by Dr. Lauretta Justin

Visit CoachJamesJustin.com or Amazon to get our products!

Table of Contents

Introduction 1

Chapter 1. The Bible is the Ultimate Authority and Guide for Christian Counseling 3

Chapter 2. The Role of the Holy Spirit in Counseling 27

Chapter 3. Understand the Path to Repentance, Healing and Transformation 55

Chapter 4. How to Prepare Yourself to Successfully Start your Christian Counseling Ministry 87

Conclusion 111

References 113

About the Authors 121

Introduction

Do you feel called to be in the counseling ministry? Do people often seek your advice? Do you feel excited and fulfilled when you help others achieve their goals? If you answered yes to any of these questions, you've picked up the right program!

Welcome you to the "Foundations of Christian Counseling Course!" We wrote this course manual to inspire you and to equip you with the essential knowledge; tools and skills you'll need to start and grow your counseling ministry.

This course serves as a foundation of Biblical-based counseling, with special attention given to tough issues that distress today's generation. Our ultimate goal is to introduce you to the Biblical answers for modern day problems. The course will provide you an overview of the resources and knowledge that apply to a broad scope of issues you'll face in your counseling ministry.

Upon successful completion of this class, you'll be able to:

1. Understand and use the Bible as the Ultimate Authority and Guide for Christian Counseling. We'll discuss the Biblical model of counseling.
2. Understand the Role of the Holy Spirit in Christian Counseling.
3. Understand the Process of Repentance, Healing and Transformation. We'll discuss major issues you'll face in your counseling ministry; and how to help your clients overcome them. Evaluate the differences between Christian counseling and secular counseling.
4. How to Prepare Yourself to Start and Grow your Christian Counseling Ministry. Identify foundational counseling skills, character and knowledge needed to develop your counseling ministry.

Chapter 1

The Bible is the Ultimate Authority and Guide for Christian Counseling

*"The Church must create an atmosphere in which the Word of God is honored and submitted to, in which human wisdom is never used to judge or qualify revelation. As far as the things of God are concerned, Christians must be totally under the teaching of Scripture and the illumination of the Holy Spirit. Only then can we be open to God's wisdom and truly **become wise**..." (John MacArthur).*

Module 1: First Thing First

Before we explore the Bible as the ultimate guide and authority for Christian Counseling, let's take five minutes to reflect and answer the following 5 questions:

1. Why do you want to become a counselor?

   _____
   _____
   _____
   _____
   _____
   _____
   _____

2. What does counseling mean to you?

   _____
   _____
   _____
   _____
   _____
   _____
   _____

3. How is the Bible relevant in solving the problems we face today?

_____
_____
_____
_____
_____
_____

4. Do you have any struggles that you feel the Bible does not directly address? If so, explain?

_____
_____
_____
_____
_____
_____

5. How can other books and resources be used in Christian counseling?

_____
_____
_____
_____
_____
_____

The Goal of Christian Counseling

The goal of Christian counseling is to help people regain a sense of hope, security and significance for their lives that is found in Jesus Christ. Christian counseling focuses on a few main principles that are different from secular counseling. It focuses on the care of the whole person. It looks at a person's spirit, soul and body. It maintains the values and principles taught in the Bible.

Christian Counseling History

The concept of *Christian Counseling* began in the late 1960s leading into the 1970s with the Nouthetic Counseling Movement directed by Jay E. Adams. Nouthetic counseling is a form of Evangelical Protestant pastoral counseling based solely upon the Bible and focused on Christ. Adams initiated this form of counseling because he did not believe in psychological practices. He taught that the Bible alone is sufficient for all counseling; and that is the central message of Christian counseling. He believed that it was the job of the church to heal people who he believed were morally corrupted, but labeled by society as mentally ill. In his book *Competent to Counsel*, he described his Christian-based approach to counseling. This method was different from the psychological and psychiatric solutions of the time.

David Powlison was another person who made Christian Counseling popular. In the 80s, he began to publish the Journal of Biblical Counseling. In this publication, he made his Christian belief known and was extremely influential in the advancement of the Nouthetic Counseling movement.

Integration of Theology and Psychology

Efforts to combine the Theology, Psychology or other scientific or academic disciplines are sometimes called "integration." Integration of academic subjects with theology has a long history in academia and continues in many colleges and universities that have continued their founding religious traditions. There are many kinds of integration. The way in which Christianity has been integrated with psychology thus far is by considering the ways in which psychology and the Bible agree and not integrating the teachings of psychology that don't agree with the Bible. Stanton Jones and Richard Buteman are popular for their writings on the concept on how to integrate Theology and Psychology.

3 Reasons why we believe that the Bible is the ultimate authority and guide for Christian counseling

Although we acknowledge that there are other theories and tools used in the field of counseling, this class will focus on the Bible as the foundational and theoretical framework for Christian Counseling. As Christians, we believe the Bible is the ultimate authority and guideline for how we ought to live on earth. It contains the wisdom and the principles for Christian Counseling and for us to live abundantly.

For us Christians, the key to live an abundant life is to follow the Word of God. We *believe* that the Bible is the inspired Word of God and the supreme authority for all matters. That is why we use it as the ultimate guide to counsel God's people.

What makes the Bible the supreme authority on all matters? How do we know that to be the truth? Here are some of the reasons why we believe that the Holy Bible is a supreme authority and guide for salvation and abundant living:

Reason #1: The Word of God bears witness of its own authority because the Old and the New Testaments Support the Authority of the Bible.

"...Every matter must be established by the testimony of two or three witnesses" (2 Corinthians s 13:1, NLT).

What's a testament? A testament is a covenant between God and humanity. It's a tangible proof or an expression of conviction. "It's a will or an act by which a person determines the disposition of his or her property after death" (Meriam-Webster Dictionary).

The word "testament" can have different meanings depending on the context, so the first thing to do is to define the word "testament" as the Bible uses it.

"For where there is a testament, there must also of necessity be the death of the testator. For a testament is in force after men are dead, since it has no power at all while the testator lives" (Hebrews 9:16-17).

From this verse we see that the Bible uses another meaning of the word "testament." It is used in the sense of "last will and testament," or as what we simply call a "will." So, the testaments are a type of will; an issue of instructions to be carried out once the creator of the will has died. Therefore, the New Testament is Christ's last will and testament for us to keep now that He has left the earth.

The word "testament" is one of multiple descriptive words used in the Bible. Therefore, the Old and New Testaments are writings that contain the "last will and testament" of God, which enables us to enter a covenant relation with Him. The central blessings of this covenant relationship include salvation and for us to have abundant life. *"The thief does not come except to steal, and to kill, and to destroy. I have come that they may have life, and that they may have it more abundantly" (John 10:10, NKJV).*

The Old Testament supports the New Testament and they are not diametrically opposed to one another; neither do they conflict with one another. For example, Jesus applied the spiritual or internal applications of the Old Testament law (See Matthew 5), not doing away with it. In other words, there are not contradictions, but simply deeper New Testament elaborations of the Old Testament. If you have the Holy Spirit of God, then you would come to understand that these differences are not contradictions, but rather like the Biblical concept of having two witnesses to verify anything being established as true. One witness was not enough, even in the Old Testament (Duet 17:6; 19:15) but "every matter may be established by the testimony of two or three witnesses" (Matt 18:16). Apostle Paul also concluded that "Every charge must be established by the evidence of two or three witnesses" (2 Corinthians s 13:1) and so the Old Testament supports and validates the New Testament. Since many verses in the New Testament quoted out of the Old Testament, it validates the Old; therefore, there is no contradiction between the two whatsoever.

New Testament Testimony of the Authority of the Old Testament

- Jesus said, "Scripture cannot be broken" (John 10:35).

- Jesus answered Satan's attacks by quoting scripture and saying "it is written" or "it stands on record" (Matthew 4:4, 7, 10).

- Old Testament scriptures are: sacred (2 Timothy 3:15), holy (Romans 1:2) inspired of God (2 Timothy 3:16), need to be read (Matthew 21:42).

Notes:
_____
_____
_____
_____
_____
_____
_____

New Testament Testimony of the Authority of the New Testament

- "All scripture is breathed of God and is profitable for teaching, correction, rebuke and training in righteousness, so that the man of God may be equipped for every good work" (2 Timothy 3:16).

- Paul said his words to them were the Word of God (1 Thessalonians 2:13; 1 Corinthians s 4:1; 2 Corinthians s 5:20).

- Important not to add or subtract from the words of this prophecy (Revelation 22:18-19).

Notes:

_____
_____
_____
_____
_____
_____
_____

In addition, let's look at what the following scriptures have to say about the Word of God:

- *"In the beginning was the Word, and the Word was with God, and the Word was God" (John 1:1, NIV).*

- *"Your word, Lord, is eternal; it stands firm in the heavens" (Psalm 119:89, NIV)*

- *"Above all, you must understand that no prophecy of Scripture came about by the prophet's own interpretation. For prophecy never had its origin in the will of man, but men spoke from God as they were carried along by the Holy Spirit" (2 Peter 1:20-21, NIV).* These scriptures show the authority of the Bible, the inspired word of God.

Reason #2: The Word of God is powerful.

- Because it judges the thoughts of our heart. *"For the word of God is alive and active. Sharper than any double-edged sword, it penetrates even to dividing soul and spirit, joints and marrow; it judges the thoughts and attitudes of the heart" (Hebrews 4:12, NIV).*

- Because with His Word, God created everything. *"In the beginning was the Word, and the Word was with God, and the Word was God. He was in the beginning with God. All things were made through Him, and without Him nothing was made that was made" (John 1:1-3).*

- Because God's word produces results. *"So shall My word be that goes forth from My mouth; It shall not return to Me void, but it shall accomplish what I please, and it shall prosper in the thing for which I sent it" (Isaiah 55:11).*

Notes:

_____
_____
_____
_____
_____
_____
_____

Reason #3: The Word of God precedes all human reasons, the church and traditions

- Human reason—*"Trust in the Lord with all your heart, and lean not on your own understanding; in all your ways acknowledge Him, And He shall direct [a] your paths. Do not be wise in your own eyes; Fear the Lord and depart from evil" (Proverbs 3:5-7).*

- The church—*"And I tell you that you are Peter, and on this rock I will build my church, and the gates of Hades will not overcome it" (Matt 16:18).*

- Traditions—*"Beware lest any man spoil you through philosophy and vain deceit, after the tradition of men, after the rudiments of the world, and not after Christ" (Col. 2:8).*

Notes:
_____
_____
_____
_____
_____
_____
_____

Quiz:

1. According to our class discussion, what is the 1st reason why we believe that the Bible is the ultimate authority on all matters?

a. Because it's the most printed book in history
b. Because the Bible bears witness of its own authority
c. Because that's what we were taught
d. Because it's a Holy Book

2. According to 2 Timothy 3:16, all scripture is breathed of God and is profitable for:

a. Teaching
b. Correction
c. Rebuke
d. All of the above

3. True or False. The New Testament testifies of the authority of the Old Testament.

a. True
b. False

4. Why do we need the written word of God, even though Jesus (The Word) lives in us through the Holy Spirit?

a. To judge the thoughts of our hearts
b. To give us reading practice
c. To give us superior knowledge
d. To make us better than the world

5. Which scripture reference helps us understand that even though the scriptures were written by humans, they are prophetic word of God?

a. 1 Corinthians s 12:1
b. 2 Peter 1:20-21
c. Psalm 119:89
d. John 3:16

Module 2: What's the primary reason why we face problems in our journey of life?

While it's God's intent for us to live abundantly, there are many problems we face in our journey of life. These problems prevent us from achieving our full potential and fulfilling our God-given purpose in life. Here are seven (7) of the most common problems you'll face in your counseling practice:

1. Marriage and Family issues
2. Depression and other Mood Disorders
3. Fear, Anxiety and Worry
4. Trauma, Grief and loss
5. Anger, Un-forgiveness, Bitterness and Personality Disorders
6. Alcohol and Drug Problems
7. Sexual problems and immorality

As previously mentioned, there are many philosophical, psychological and sociological theories on the cause of humanity's problems. For example, the philosopher Pascal claims that *"All of humanity's problems stem from man's inability to sit quietly in a room alone" (Blaise Pascal, Pensées)*. But for us Christians, we believe that the source of all human problems come from SIN. "For everyone has sinned; we all fall short of God's glorious standard" (Romans 3:23, NLT).

What is sin? It's the breaking of God's law. *"A sin is any thought or action that falls short of God's will. God is perfect and anything we do that falls short of His perfection is sin" (Billy Graham)*. If God says, "Do not lie" and we lie, then we have broken His law and have sinned. When we sin, we offend God because it is His law that we have broken.
The problem with sin is that it broke our relationship and fellowship with God. Read Genesis 1 for more details. As a result of sin, humanity became imperfect.

The reality is that sin hurts us. *"For the wages of sin is death, but the free gift of God is eternal life through Christ Jesus our Lord" (Romans 6:23, NLT).* Sin is like a beast that seeks to devour and destroy the beauty of God's kingdom. Ultimately, sin is our blatant determination to make life work on our own, and to find life apart from an intimate, dependent relationship with the Lord of life.

The solution to sin is repentance. *"Repentance is to turn from sin and dedicate oneself to the amendment of one's life, to feel regret and to change one's mind, feeling and action" (Merriam-Webster Dictionary).* Repentance comes from conviction through the word of God by faith. The Bible calls us to repent so that we can be saved. *"Now repent of your sins and turn to God, so that your sins may be wiped away"* (Acts 3:19, NLT).

So, with all this talk about sin and repentance, how does any of this apply in the 21st century? According to Biblestudytools.com, *"People aren't reading the Bible because they think it is irrelevant to everyday life. Many people, even those who read the Bible, do not see the Scriptures as containing instruction and answers that deal with the everyday problems they face. They think of the Bible as they would a cookbook. It is a wonderful thing for putting together thirty-person dinner parties, but it doesn't have any recipes in it for tonight's dinner for the family. It's great for special occasions but not for everyday situations."* The reality is that the Bible is still relevant today because sin is still sin, and God still remains in His throne.

As long as humans exist, sin will exist; and as long as there is sin, the Bible will remain relevant. God's word is the ultimate guide to an ultimate life. The solution to our sin problem is available in Jesus Christ. Jesus offered himself as the sacrificial lamb to save us from sin and eternal death. He became the pathway to our salvation and eternal life. His purpose is for us to have life and have it more abundantly (John 10:10). This abundant life begins here on earth right now! If you believe in Him and follow His life principles, you'll have abundant life, success, joy and happiness.

It's important to recognize and accept that our issues come as a result of our sins, and the word of God is the only weapon strong enough to defeat the power of sin. The Christian counselor must acknowledge the absolute authority of God's word and it's principles as the ultimate guide for a transformed life.

Notes:

_____
_____
_____
_____
_____
_____
_____

Reflections:

1. Are there areas in your life where you're still trying to make it on your own without depending on the Lord? If so explain.

_____
_____
_____
_____
_____
_____
_____

2. In your own words, write down what you'd say to the Lord about how you've been managing this area of your life. A prayer of repentance.

_____
_____
_____
_____
_____
_____
_____

3. What would you want the Lord to do to help you in this area?

_____
_____
_____
_____
_____
_____
_____

4. Write down the name of at least one person that you're going to ask to pray with you and keep you accountable in this area.

_____
_____
_____
_____
_____
_____
_____

Module 3: 7 Popular Counseling Theories

As a counselor, it's important to be aware of various theories, models and techniques of counseling. When you are aware of the available tools, you'll be prepared in determining the most effective ones. This course focuses on the Biblical perspective of counseling. However, we'll also introduce you to other theories of counseling. According to basic-counseling-skills.com, the most popular modern counseling theories are as follows:

1. Psychoanalytic Therapy (Sigmund Freud)

Psychoanalytic therapy is a type of treatment based upon the theories of Sigmund Freud, who is considered one of the forefathers of psychology and the founder of psychoanalysis. This therapy explores how the unconscious mind influences thoughts and behaviors, with the aim of offering insight and resolution to the person seeking therapy.

Psychoanalytic therapy tends to look at experiences from early childhood to see if these events have affected the individual's life, or potentially contributed to current concerns. This form of therapy is considered a long-term choice and can continue for weeks, months or even years depending on the depth of the concern being explored.

Differing from several other therapy types, psychoanalytic therapy aims to make deep-seated changes in personality and emotional development.

Notes:

_____
_____
_____
_____
_____

2. Person-Centered Therapy (PCT)

This form of talk-psychotherapy was developed by psychologist Carl Rogers in the 1940s and 1950s. The goal of PCT is to provide clients with an opportunity to develop a sense of self where they can realize how their attitudes, feelings and behavior are being negatively affected.

The counselor provides the growth-promoting climate, and the client is then free and able to discover and grow as she/he wants and needs to. Prevailing characteristics of the session are active listening, empathy, acceptance (unconditional positive regard) and genuineness.

Notes:

_____
_____
_____
_____
_____
_____
_____

3. Holistic Health (Biopsychosocial) Therapy

The Biopsychosocial Therapy (BPS) assumes as a fact that biological, psychological (thoughts, emotions, and behaviors), and social factors all play a significant role in human functioning. This model of therapy was first formulated by Dr. George L. Engels. He believes that we all have physical, intellectual, social, emotional and vocational needs. The neglect of these needs reduces our ability to withstand the effects of stress and to maintain wellbeing.

Notes:

_____
_____
_____
_____
_____
_____
_____

4. Strengths-Based Therapy

This method of counseling focuses on what is going right in a person's life. It's linked to Positive psychology and the science of happiness and human strengths formulated by Alan Carr. In this method of counseling, the counselor and client work together to find past and present strengths, successes and use these to address current and future challenges. Its first cousin, Positive Thinking or Learned Optimism, is about learning a positive perspective—focusing on what can go right instead of what can go wrong.

Notes:

_____
_____
_____
_____
_____
_____
_____

5. Cognitive Behavioral Therapy (CBT or ABC Method)

Two of the earliest forms of Cognitive Behavioral Therapy were Rational Emotive Behavior Therapy (REBT), developed by Albert Ellis in the 1950s, and Cognitive Therapy, developed by Aaron T. Beck in the 1960s.

It's a form of psychotherapy. It was originally designed to treat depression, but is now used for a number of conditions such as mood, anxiety, personality, eating, addiction, dependence, tic, and psychotic disorders.

The goal of Cognitive Behavioral Therapy is not to diagnose a person with a particular disease, but to look at them as a whole and decide what needs to be fixed. The basic steps in a Cognitive-Behavioral Assessment include:

Step 1: Identify critical behaviors

Step 2: Determine whether critical behaviors are excesses or deficits

Step 3: Evaluate critical behaviors for frequency, duration, or intensity (obtain a baseline)

Step 4: If critical behavior is in excess, attempt to decrease frequency, duration, or intensity of behaviors; but if critical behavior is in deficit, attempt to increase behaviors.

Notes:
_____
_____
_____
_____
_____
_____
_____

6. Solution-Focused Brief Therapy (SFBT)

SFBT is an evidenced-based psychotherapy approach that was developed by Steve De Shazer during the late 1970's. This method of counseling focuses on what clients want to achieve through the therapy rather than on the problem(s) that made them seek help. The approach does not focus on the past, but instead focuses on the present and future. The client is asked to envision how the future will be different when the problem is no longer present.

Notes:

___

7. The Existential Therapy (Why Am I Here?)

Existential psychotherapy is a philosophical method of therapy that operates on the belief that inner conflict within a person is due to that individual's conflict with the givens of existence. This therapeutic approach focuses on the meaning of the present life. Viktor Frankyl is one the foremost leader of this approach. He said, "He who knows the 'why' for his existence, will be able to bear almost any 'how.'" The goal of this therapy is to define one's identity and establishing meaningful relationships with oneself and others to solve ones problems.

Notes:

___

Quiz:

1. Which of the following is not a prevailing characteristic of client centered counseling?

   a. Active listening
   b. Sympathy
   c. Acceptance
   d. Genuineness

2. Which counseling theory focuses on what is going right in a person's life?

   a. Psychoanalytic Theory
   b. Feel Good Theory
   c. Solution Focused Therapy
   d. Strength Based Theory

3. True or False: In solution focused therapy, the client is asked to envision how the future will be different when the problem is no longer present.

   a. True
   b. False

4. According to this lecture, who is the founding father of Cognitive Behavior Therapy?

   a. Sigmund Freud
   b. Carl Jung
   c. Albert Ellis, PhD
   d. Wilhelm Wundt

5. How is Christian counseling different from Holistic Biopsychosocial Counseling?

   a. Christian counseling does not focus on physical health, whereas Holistic counseling does.

b. Christian counseling is only done in church, whereas Holistic counseling is done in secular settings.
c. Holistic counseling claims that an imbalanced life is the source of bio-psycho-social issues, whereas Christian counseling claims that sin is the source of our issues.
d. Holistic counseling does not support spiritual development, whereas Christian counseling does.

Chapter 2

The Role of the Holy Spirit in Counseling

"If the Holy Spirit is the primary counselor, then Biblical counseling is not merely a dialogue between a counselor and a counselee. Rather it is a trialogue in which a counselor participates in the Holy Spirit's work already underway in the counselee" (Justin Holcomb and Mike Wilkerson, headhearthand.org).

Module 1: Who is the Holy Spirit?

The identity of the Holy Spirit has been misunderstood by many people. Some view the Holy Spirit as a mystical force. Others understand the Holy Spirit as the impersonal power that God makes available to followers of Christ.

For us Christians, we believe that the Holy Spirit is God. The Holy Spirit is referred to as the Lord and Giver of Life. He is The Creator Spirit, present before the creation of the universe and through His power everything was made in Jesus Christ, by God the Father. According to CBN.com, the Holy Spirit is the third person of the trinity, which Christians refer to as God. He is no more, no less God than the person referred to in the Bible as Jehovah: God the Father, or Jesus Christ: God the son. He is fully divine, a distinct individual, and active in the world to convict us of our need for God, as well as comfort, teach and lead us in the direction of God's will.

What does the Bible say about the identity of the Holy Spirit? Simply put, the Holy Spirit *is* our God. *The Holy Spirit is* clearly identified in the scriptures as God. The Holy Spirit is mentioned on equal level with God (carm.org/christianity/christian-doctrine/verses-showing-identity-ministry-and-personhood-holy-spirit). The following Biblical verses show the identity of the Holy Spirit:

- Matthew 28:19, *"Go therefore and make disciples of all the nations, baptizing them in the name of the Father and the Son and the Holy Spirit."*

- 2 Corinthians 3:16-18, *"but whenever a man turns to the Lord, the veil is taken away. Now the Lord is the Spirit; and where the Spirit of the Lord is, there is liberty. But we all, with unveiled face beholding as in a mirror the glory of the Lord, are being transformed into the same image from glory to glory, just as from the Lord, the Spirit."*

- 2 Corinthians 13:14, *"The grace of the Lord Jesus Christ, and the love of God, and the fellowship of the Holy Spirit, be with you all."*

- Ephesians 4:4-6, *"There is one body and one Spirit, just as also you were called in one hope of your calling; one Lord, one faith, one baptism, one God and Father of all who is over all and through all and in all."*

The Holy Spirit is a divine, a being with a mind, emotions and a will. We know that the Holy Spirit is indeed a divine person because He possesses a mind, emotions and a will. The Holy Spirit thinks and knows (1 Corinthians 2:10). The Holy Spirit can be grieved (Ephesians 4:30). The Spirit intercedes for us (Romans 8:26-27). He makes decisions according to His will (1 Corinthians 12:7-11).

The *Holy Spirit is omnipresence as written in Psalm 139:7-8, "Where can I go from your Spirit? Where can I flee from your presence? If I go up to the heavens, you are there; if I make my bed in the depths, you are there."*

In 1 Corinthians 2:10, we see the characteristic of omniscience in the Holy Spirit. "But God has revealed it to us by his Spirit. The Spirit searches all things, even the deep things of God. For who among men knows the thoughts of a man except the man's spirit within him? In the same way no one knows the thoughts of God except the Spirit of God."

The Holy Spirit knows all things. The fact that the Holy Spirit is God is clearly seen in many Scriptures, including Acts 5:3-4. In this verse, Peter confronts Ananias as to why he lied to the Holy Spirit, and tells him that he had "not lied to men but to God." It is a clear declaration that lying to the Holy Spirit is lying to God.

Notes:

_____
_____
_____
_____
_____
_____
_____

Names and Titles of the Holy Spirit

In the Bible, we find different names and titles of the Holy Spirit. **Above all, the Holy Spirit is our "Comforter, Counselor and Advocate"** (Isaiah 11:2; John 14:16; 15:26; 16:7). All three words are translations of the Greek word *Parakletos*, from which we get the word "Paraclete," another name for the Spirit.

The Holy Spirit is the Comforter, Counselor and Advocate that Jesus promised. When Jesus went away to Heaven, His disciples were greatly distressed because they had lost His comforting presence. But He promised to send the Holy Spirit to comfort, console, and guide those who belong to Him. *"It is best for you that I go away, because if I don't, the*

Advocate won't come. If I do go away, then I will send him to you" (John 16:7, 15:26 & 14:16, 26, NLT).

Here are some other names and titles of the Holy Spirit as described in the Bible:

- **Guide:** Just as the Holy Spirit guided the writers of the Bible to record the truth, so does He promise to guide believers to know and understand that truth (John 16:13). God's truth is "foolishness" to the world, because it is "spiritually discerned" (1 Corinthians 2:14). Those who belong to Christ have the indwelling Spirit who guides us into all we need to know in regard to spiritual matters. Those who do not belong to Christ have no "interpreter" to guide them to know and understand God's Word. As you continue to read, pray and meditate on God's word, you'll have a clearer understanding of the Scriptures and the Holy Spirit.

- **Intercessor:** The person who intervenes on behalf of another. The Holy Spirit is our intercessor. One of the most encouraging and comforting aspects of the Holy Spirit is His ministry of intercession on behalf of those He inhabits (Romans 8:26). Because we often don't know what or how to pray when we approach God, the Spirit intercedes and prays for us. He intercedes for us "with wordless groans," so that when we are oppressed and overwhelmed by trials and the cares of life, He comes alongside to lend assistance as He sustains us before the throne of grace. For more information on the subject of prayer and intercession, read "Express Yourself," a book we published in 2011.

- **Teacher:** Jesus promised that the Holy Spirit would teach His disciples "all things" and bring to their remembrance the things He said while He was with them (John 14:26 & 1 Corinthians 2:13). The writers of the New Testament were moved by the Spirit to remember and understand the instructions Jesus gave for the building and organizing of the Church, the doctrines regarding Himself, the directives for holy living and the revelation of things to come.

- **Witness:** The Holy Spirit is called "witness" because He verifies and testifies to the fact that we are children of God, that Jesus and the disciples who performed miracles were sent by God, and that the books of the Bible are divinely inspired (Romans 8:16; Hebrews 2:4; 10:15). Further, the Holy Spirit is a witness by giving the gifts of the Spirit to believers, He witnesses to us and the world that we belong to God (gotquestions.org/names-Holy-Spirit.html).

When Jesus went away to Heaven, His disciples were greatly distressed because they had lost His comforting presence. But He promised to send the Holy Spirit to comfort, console, and guide those who belong to Him. The Holy Spirit also "bears witness" with our spirits that we belong to Christ; and thereby assure us of salvation.

Notes:

_____
_____
_____
_____
_____
_____

3 Misconceptions about the Holy Spirit

1. The Holy Spirit is there only to make me feel good and all tingly inside. After His baptism, the Holy Spirit entered Jesus gently, deftly, exquisitely—with the soft

movements of a descending dove. But what did the Holy Spirit do next? And the Spirit immediately led him out into the wilderness (Mark 1:12). The Holy Spirit can use any event or experience to help us develop and grow. So don't expect the Holy Spirit to coddle you—not if you want to grow spiritually. The Holy Spirit understands that we learn best against the odds, in hardship, in the hostile desert rather than along the peaceful banks of the Jordan River.

Notes:

_____
_____
_____
_____
_____
_____
_____

2. We can rejoice, too, when we run into problems and trials, for we know that they help us develop endurance. And endurance develops strength of character, and character strengthens our confident hope of salvation. And this hope will not lead to disappointment. For we know how dearly God loves us, because he has given us the Holy Spirit to fill our hearts with His love (Romans 5:3-5 & James 1:2-5, NLT).

Notes:

_____
_____
_____
_____
_____
_____
_____

The Holy Spirit comes and goes; we need to cry out for Him to come. He is only available to a chosen few.
In the old covenant the Holy Spirit rested on certain people for certain times. But in the new covenant He abides with us and "makes His home in us" (2 Timothy 1:14, AMP). If you have received the Holy Spirit, be comforted, for He's not going anywhere. He has promised to never leave nor forsake us (Hebrews 13:5).

According to Galatians 3:14, Jesus redeemed us so that we might receive the blessings promised to Abraham; namely, the promise of the Holy Spirit. Do you believe that Jesus has redeemed you? Then you are eligible to receive the promised Holy Spirit.

Who is not eligible to accept Him? The unsaved world, "because it neither sees Him nor knows Him."*The Spirit of truth, whom the world cannot receive, because it neither sees Him nor knows Him; but you know Him, for He dwells with you and will be in you" (John 14:17).*

Look at what Peter said to those who heard the gospel at Pentecost: *"Repent and be baptized, every one of you, in the name of Jesus Christ for the forgiveness of your sins. And you will receive the gift of the Holy Spirit" (Acts 2:38).* The Holy Spirit does not limit Himself to a chosen few. Believe in Jesus and you will, you will, you will receive the promised Gift! Believe it!

Notes:
_____
_____
_____
_____
_____
_____
_____

3. To receive the Holy Spirit, you must fast, pray, and work real hard.

While reading the Bible, meditating, praying and working hard have many benefits in life, they are not enough to receive the Holy Spirit. The Holy Spirit is a free gift from Jesus Christ to His children. We simply need to ask and receive the Holy Spirit by faith (Galatians 3:14).

The Holy Spirit is the best gift that Jesus sent to all His children. He knows that we need the best gift to keep us safe and secure while we are in this world. *"If you then, though you are evil, know how to give good gifts to your children, how much more will your Father in heaven give the Holy Spirit to those who ask Him!" (Luke 11:13, NIV).* Here Jesus is saying that the Holy Spirit is freely given to all who ask. Don't let anyone tell you that you must *do stuff* to earn what God freely gives. Jesus already did it all. *"Until now you have not asked for anything in my name. Ask and you will receive, and your joy will be complete"* (John 16:24, NIV). Everything you need from God, simply ask and believe; and you shall receive it according to His perfect will!

Notes:
_____
_____
_____
_____
_____
_____
_____

Quiz:

Instruction: Circle the best answer according to the letter of this course.

1. Which of the following name and/or title of the Holy Spirit is not Biblically correct?

   a. Guide
   b. Counselor
   c. Director
   d. Teacher

2. We can know that the Holy Spirit is indeed a divine person because He possesses:

   a. A mind
   b. Emotions
   c. A will
   d. All of the above

3. According to this lecture, which is one of the most encouraging and comforting aspects of the Holy Spirit?

   a. Intercessor
   b. Teacher
   c. Guide
   d. Counselor

4. What can we infer from the following statement: *Don't expect the Holy Spirit to coddle you—not if you want to grow spiritually.*

   a. If I'm not going through a hard time right now, the Holy Spirit is not with me.
   b. The Holy Spirit is always looking for new ways to make me suffer.

c. The Holy Spirit is mean.
d. Even though one of the roles of the Holy Spirit is a comforter, it does not mean that I'll always feel comfortable.

5. True or False - To receive the Holy Spirit you must fast, pray and work real hard to be holy.

a. True
b. False

Module 2: How to Distinguish the Voice of the Holy Spirit

Is it possible to hear the voice of the Holy Spirit? Jesus told His disciples, *"But when he, the Spirit of truth, comes, he will guide you into all the truth. He will not speak on his own; he will speak only what he hears, and he will tell you what is yet to come"* (John 16:13). The Holy Spirit is available to those who have put their trust in Jesus Christ. He speaks to our hearts and leads us in the right direction when we learn to listen.

The Holy Spirit has been described as wind (John 3:8), a dove (Mark 1:10), and a gift (Acts 2:38). The Spirit of God can be grieved and quenched by disobedient believers. It is possible to hear the voice of the Spirit when believers humble themselves to:

1. Be Quiet

"Come with me by yourselves to a quiet place and get some rest" (Mark 6:31). We are sometimes too busy to hear the voice of the Holy Spirit. He is gentle and patiently waits for us to hunger for His presence in our lives. Being quiet before the Lord is more than just not talking. It's quieting your anxious thoughts and meditating on His word as you wait to hear from the Holy Spirit. We need to find a good place where we can sit before God uninterrupted by other distractions. Meditation is a great way that we can quiet ourselves to listen to hear the voice of the Holy Spirit. Meditation does not have to be long and complicated. If you are new to meditation, you can start with one minute per day to meditate on your favorite Bible verse.

Notes:

_____
_____
_____

_____
_____
_____
_____

2. Be Prepared

"Prepare the way for the Lord, make straight paths for him" (Mark 1:3). We must take the time to reflect on our thoughts, words, feelings, and actions if we want to hear from God. The goal is to develop the mind of Christ so that we can be receptive to hear from the Holy Spirit.

Our sins keep us from hearing the quiet voice of the Holy Spirit. By confessing and repenting of our sins, we allow the Spirit of God to come into our hearts that has been cleansed by the Lord. The more we grow in our relationship with God, the more sensitive we become to the presence of sin. Prepare yourself to hear from the Holy Spirit by studying, meditating and practicing God's word.

Notes:

_____
_____
_____
_____
_____
_____
_____

3. Be Aware

Jesus said, "If you hold to my teaching, you are really my disciples. Then you will know the truth, and the truth will set you free" (John 8:31-32). It's difficult to hear from the Holy Spirit when we don't know the Bible. We are most familiar with the word of God through the hearing and teaching of it. Also, through personal memorization, meditation, and personal study, believers can know the truths of God's word. Everything the Holy Spirit speaks to our hearts will align perfectly with Scripture. Through consistent exposure to the Bible, we will gain greater confidence in hearing the voice of the Spirit.

Notes:

_____
_____
_____
_____
_____
_____
_____
_____

4. Be Open

"Now faith is confidence in what we hope for and assurance about what we do not see" (Hebrews 11:1). Faith is the foundation of our walk with God. We can only hear and please God in faith. *"But without faith it is impossible to please Him, for he who comes to God must believe that He is, and that He is a rewarder of those who diligently seek Him"* (Hebrews 11:6). We believe in Him even though we can't see or touch the Holy Spirit. Our faith is demonstrated by our solid trust that God will lead us in the right direction even in times of the unknown. There needs to be an openness coupled with courage to stepping out in faith when following the direction of the Holy Spirit. The opportunity of faith emboldens us to grow up spiritually and become more acquainted with the voice of the Spirit.

Notes:

_____
_____
_____
_____
_____

5. Be Ready

"Remind the people to be subject to rulers and authorities, to be obedient, to be ready to do whatever is good, to slander no one, to be peaceable and considerate, and always to be gentle toward everyone" (Titus 3:1-2). Our faith in the Holy Spirit is evident when we are ready to obey even when it's inconvenient. The readiness to follow in obedience gives us the assurance that we are moving in the right direction. The Holy Spirit empowers the obedient with great strength and peace in the midst of difficulty. Believers who hear from God make it a practice of their lives to obey His word. **It's not always easy to obey God's word, but if you're willing, He'll help you. If you need help to follow God, you can ask Him in prayer.**

Notes:
_____
_____
_____
_____
_____
_____
_____

6. Be Patient

"Therefore, as God's chosen people, holy and dearly loved, clothe yourselves with compassion, kindness, humility, gentleness and patience" (Colossians 3:12). Hearing from the Holy Spirit requires us to be patient and wait. The Holy Spirit can't be rushed into our life situations. He knows the whole story from beginning to end and will move in the appointed time. We need to seek His peace and learn to wait on the Lord with an attitude of expectancy, not complacency.

Notes:
_____
_____
_____
_____
_____
_____
_____

The voice of the Holy Spirit is gentle and quiet—very difficult for us to hear when we don't pay close attention. We are connected to the Lord through the Holy Spirit allowing the sweetest communion. By choosing to humble ourselves in being quiet, prepared, aware, open, read, and patient, we will hear His voice more clearly and we will trust Him more freely. The Holy Spirit is a gift of God's grace to His people. Open your gift wisely and be blessed in His presence (whatchristianswanttoknow.com/how-to-hear-the-voice-of-the-holy-spirit-in-your-life).

Quiz:

1. True/False - Everything the Holy Spirit speaks to our hearts will mostly line up with Scripture.

   a. True
   b. False

2. What are some of the ways believers can learn the truths of the word of God?

   a. Scripture memorization
   b. Meditation
   c. Personal study
   d. All of the above

3. How can we trust that God will lead us in the right direction even in times of the unknown?

   a. By going to many ministry meetings
   b. By attending classes at Faith Christian University (FCU)
   c. By believing and relying on the leading of the Holy Spirit
   d. By being involved in ministry

4. How can you be quiet before the Lord?

   a. By not talking
   b. By quieting your anxious thoughts
   c. By meditating on His word
   d. All of the above

5. Which of the following isn't a necessary step to hear the voice of the Spirit?

a. Be quiet
b. Be open
c. Be patient
d. Be charismatic

Module 3: How the Holy Spirit Helps in Counseling

The Holy Spirit is our partner in the counseling process. He can use the knowledge, skills and abilities we have to help others. He takes the tools we have learned from real life experiences, sciences and teaches us how to translate them into a higher realm of spiritual insight. Specifically, if we have an ear to hear what the Spirit says, He will teach us how to take what we have learned about human development, mental health, diagnosis and counseling techniques to a new level.

At the same time, the Holy Spirit is functioning in the mind of the counselor, He is also at work in the mind of the counselee. Jesus said, "And when he is come, he will reprove the world of sin, and of righteousness, and of judgment" (John 16:8, KJV). As you compassionately and lovingly confront the counselee with the circumstances that brought him to you, you can rely on the Holy Spirit to create uncomfortable levels of tension within the counselee that will motivate him to make the redemptive changes Jesus wants him to make, and to find the healing and deliverance he needs.

At the same time, you can count on the Holy Spirit to give you the inner strength necessary to tolerate increasingly intense levels of stress created by the counselee's conflicting attempts to simultaneously escape from and deal with his spiritual and emotional pain. Without the ability to deal with your own mounting levels of anxiety, your need for comfort may lead you to retreat from issues in the person's life that need to be pressed further. At that point the limits of your comfort level interfere with the mounting level of stress needed for motivating change in the counselee. Allowing the Holy Spirit to help you build your tolerance for rising levels of tension when facing difficult counseling moments will make you more effective in precipitating the redemptive changes Christ wants to bring to your counselees.

Remember, until the pain of remaining the same hurts more than the pain of change, people will prefer to remain the same. Intolerable levels of pain are essential in moving people from where they are to where the Lord wants them to be. Developing a higher tolerance for conflict and stress than your counselees will enable you to move them compassionately through the difficult season of life that prompted them to seek your help. During those uncomfortable moments in this process, it is comforting to know that people can deal with unpleasant certainty easier than they can deal with uncertainty. Successful counseling moves people through uncertainty to certainty. May the Lord continue strengthen you as you counsel God's people!

Notes:

_____
_____
_____
_____
_____
_____
_____
_____
_____
_____
_____
_____
_____
_____
_____
_____

The gifts of the Holy Spirit

The gifts of the Holy Spirit are valuable resources for counseling. The Apostle Paul described 9 gifts of the Holy Spirit in the Bible (1 Corinthians 12:7–12). These gifts are available to all God's children. We divided these gifts into 3 sets of which equal to the 9 spiritual gifts. They are as follows:

- Gifts of the mind include the *word of wisdom*, *word of knowledge* and *discerning of spirits*.

- There are verbal gifts: *diverse kinds of tongues*, *interpretation of tongues* and *prophecy*.

- Finally, there are the power gifts: *faith*, *working of miracles* and *healing*.

All of these gifts supernaturally enrich the counseling process. When we combine our natural gifts with the supernatural gifts of the Holy Spirit, we'll create supernatural breakthrough for our clients! Therefore, a Biblical understanding of how these gifts function in the counseling relationship can enable us to be more effective counselors.

How to Use the Gifts of the Holy Spirit in Counseling

Discerning spirits

Discernment is the ability to judge well. It's the perception in the absence of judgment with a view to obtaining spiritual direction and understanding. The gift of discernment empowers you to understand your clients' thinking, feelings and behaviors. Often our clients are not able to articulate their pains, needs and wants; and we need to rely on the gift of discernment to assess their problems quickly.

The gifts of the mind can greatly enhance the diagnostic process. A trained clinician develops skill in using visual, auditory and tactile senses in diagnosing a person's problems. When the gift of discerning of spirits becomes part of this process, it takes your diagnostic skill to a new level. It allows you to discern the revealed factors or spiritual forces preventing your client's success, joy and wellbeing.

The secular approach to counseling sees a person's current mental activity as the natural outgrowth of the interaction between and among his personal history, the present circumstances of his life and the neurochemical processes of his brain. There is often no acknowledgment of any spiritual impact on this process. Although Christian counselors acknowledge the important role these natural elements play in a person's mental activity and well being, we believe one's spirit largely drives the mental process as well.

Notes:

_____
_____
_____
_____
_____
_____
_____

Word of knowledge

Excellent clinicians become experts in connecting the dots of a person's history to get the picture the person presents. However, a word of knowledge from the Holy Spirit about the person amplifies these skills. Such a word often makes its way into the mind of the counselor as an intuition or hunch.
This is why a counselor needs to exercise care in determining how and when he introduces such a word to the counselee. The counselor should never impose this word of knowledge on the counselee. Presenting it as a suggestion gives the counselee an opportunity to accept it or reject it.

Notes:

_____
_____
_____
_____
_____
_____
_____

Word of wisdom

Anyone counseling people knows there are critical moments in your care of them. As a counselor, you acquire a natural wisdom for managing times like these. However, the Christian counselor is not limited to the natural wisdom that comes from experience and counseling theories. Apostle James reminds us that wisdom is available from God to those who are humble enough to ask for it. "If any of you lack wisdom, let him ask of God who gives to all liberally" (James 1:5).

However, there is a special word of wisdom that the Holy Spirit can give us in clinical moments when we need His guidance. It alters what we would normally say or do. In retrospect, we easily recognize its divine origin by the healing impact its implementation has on the counselee.

Notes:
_____
_____
_____
_____
_____
_____
_____

Tongues, interpretation and prophecy

These verbal gifts put at the counselor's disposal a level of fluency beyond his natural ability. This is especially helpful in disciplining and directing the counselor's dialogue with the counselee.

The private gift of speaking in other tongues provides the counselor a delightful means of debriefing himself after each session. During this time he can release tensions and stress from previous sessions to the Lord that would be difficult to articulate. He may also use this personal gift to make intercession for his counselees according to the will of God (Romans 8:26, 27).

Notes:

_____
_____
_____
_____
_____
_____
_____

Faith, working of miracles, and gifts of healing

"Faith is the substance of things hoped for, the evidence of things not seen" (Hebrews 11:1, KJV). If Christian counselors are to be effective, they must be people of faith. Even secular counselors must be able to inspire hope in people. It is through faith and by grace that we are able to connect with God spiritually.

Notice the relationship between faith and hope. Faith grows out of hope. One of the early priorities in the counseling process is to inspire hope in the counselee. Hope inspired by the Holy Spirit can give birth to a gift of faith that enables both counselor and counselee to believe that the desired recovery will become a reality.

In addition, the Holy Spirit distributes gifts of healing to our counselees. Although, as Christian counselors we play our part in the process of bringing people to healing, we recognize the gift of healing that comes to our counselees is from the Holy Spirit—not from us.

Notes:

_____
_____

Christ-centered counseling requires more than devoted Christians who are expertly trained in the field of professional counseling. It is the infusion of the presence of Christ and the Holy Spirit into the counseling process that makes Christian counseling, Christ-centered (enrichmentjournal.ag.org). Christ-centered counseling is based on the teachings of Jesus Christ found in the Holy Bible.

Reflections:

1. When you think of the Holy Spirit, what comes to your mind?

_____
_____
_____
_____
_____
_____
_____
_____

2. What are some of your misconceptions about the Holy Spirit?

_____
_____
_____
_____
_____
_____
_____
_____

3. Think back to a time in your life when you heard the voice of the Holy Spirit. How did you know it was the Holy Spirit and not just your own mind?

_____
_____
_____
_____
_____
_____
_____
_____

4. Do you sometimes feel that the Holy Spirit is not with you? If so how?

_____
_____
_____
_____
_____
_____
_____
_____

5. As a counselor you will need to rely on the leading of the Holy Spirit when you counsel people. How do you need God's help in this area?

_____
_____
_____
_____
_____
_____
_____
_____
_____

Chapter 3

Understand the Path to Repentance, Healing and Transformation

"The thief comes only in order to steal and kill and destroy. I came that they may have and enjoy life, and have it in abundance [to the full, till it overflows]" (John 10:10, AMP).

Module 1: Why people do what they do

It's God's purpose that all his children have an awesome life and enjoy it more abundantly. He wants us to grow and enjoy the fruit of the Holy Spirit. "The fruit of the Spirit [the result of His presence within us] is love [unselfish concern for others], joy, [inner] peace, patience [not the ability to wait, but how we act while waiting], kindness, goodness, faithfulness, gentleness, self-control. Against such things there is no law. (Galatians 5:22-23, AMP).

It's true that we do not know and understand all the reasons why people do what they do and why we face trials and tribulations on earth. However, we believe that sin is the major reason. We described sin in detail in chapter 1.

When God created Adam and Eve—the first human beings—they were perfect. They faced no trials or tribulations. They had zero problems. They had a perfect relationship and fellowship with God.

Through disobedience, sin entered the world. Adam, Eve and their offspring became sinners, and we became disconnected from our heavenly father. We began to experience the consequences of sin. *"For the wages of sin is death, but the gift of God is eternal life in Christ Jesus our Lord" (Romans 6:23).*

Since the fall of humanity, we all want to fulfill the void inside. We use all kinds of means to do so with no success. Some people abuse substances to fill their void. Others abuse sex to fulfill their needs, only to feel empty again and again. We try to fill a void that was created for God with earthly things. That's just not going to work.

What's the biggest obstacle preventing you from enjoying life?

Notes:

_____
_____
_____
_____
_____
_____
_____
_____

What motivates our behaviors

Much research has been conducted to determine human needs and what motivates our thinking, feelings and actions. The most popular theories are as follows: Maslow's Hierarchy of Needs, Piaget's Cognitive Development and Erickson's Psychosocial Development. The idea is that if we can understand our needs, we can find ways to effectively fulfill them. Let's briefly review these 3 theories.

Maslow's Hierarchy of Needs

The most popular finding on motivations and human needs came from Abraham Maslow's work. Maslow was an American Psychologist. While each person is unique, we all share similar basic needs. Whether we know it or not, most of our behaviors are driven by those needs. According to Abraham Maslow there are 6 basic human needs that drive our thoughts, feelings and actions.

Notes:

_____
_____
_____
_____
_____
_____
_____

1. Physiological Needs:

These needs are required for our basic survival, and include breathing, food, water, sleep, sex, internal physiological balance and waste removal. If these requirements are not met, the human body cannot function properly and will ultimately fail. Physiological needs are thought to be the most important and the most basic. If those needs are not met, the human body will die before its appointed time.

Notes:

_____
_____
_____
_____
_____
_____
_____

2. Safety and Security Needs:

Security needs are important for survival, but they are not as demanding as the physiological needs. Examples of security needs include a desire for steady employment, health care, safe neighborhoods and shelter from the environment. The needs become a bit more complex at this point in the hierarchy. Now that the more basic survival needs have been fulfilled, people begin to feel that they need more control and order to their lives. A safe place to live, financial security, physical safety and staying healthy are all concerns that might come into play at this stage.

Notes:

_____
_____
_____
_____
_____
_____
_____

3. Love, Acceptance and Belonging Needs:

We all have the need to be loved and accepted from others. Also, we have the need to love and accept others. These are our interpersonal needs; and they involve feelings of belonging, connection, loving and developing Intimacy. Maslow described these needs as less basic than physiological and security needs. Relationships such as friendships, romantic attachments and families help fulfill this need for companionship and acceptance. The active participation in social, community and religious groups plays a major role in fulfilling our needs of **Love, Acceptance and Belonging**.

Notes:

_____
_____
_____
_____
_____
_____
_____

4. Esteem Need:

All humans have a need to feel respected. This includes the need for self-esteem, self-respect and self-confidence. Esteem encompasses the typical human desire to be accepted and valued by others. People often engage in a profession or hobby to gain recognition. These activities give the person a sense of contribution or value. After the first three needs have been satisfied, esteem needs becomes increasingly important. Satisfying this need and gaining acceptance and esteem helps people become more confident. Failing to gain recognition for accomplishments, however, can lead to feelings of failure or inferiority.

Notes:

_____
_____
_____
_____
_____
_____
_____

5. Finding Purpose Need:

This level of need refers to a person's full potential, and the realization of that potential. Maslow describes this level as the desire to accomplish everything that one can, to become the most that one can be. According to Maslow, *"What a man can be, he must be."* Self-actualizing people are self-aware, concerned with personal and professional growth, less concerned with the opinions of others, and interested in fulfilling their potential and purpose."

Notes:

_____
_____
_____

_____
_____
_____
_____

6. Spiritual Connection to God:

In his later years, Maslow added the sixth need. He realized that the "self" only finds its actualization in its giving to some higher goal outside oneself, in altruism and spirituality. This is the highest level of Maslow's hierarchy of needs.

In review of the 3 basic human needs, we group these needs in the following categories:

1. Spirit (the need to discover purpose and to connect with God spiritually)

2. Soul (the need for love, belonging, esteem and confidence)

3. Body (the need for water, food, air, shelter, safety and security)

Jean Piaget's Cognitive Development (1896-1980)

This theory introduced the concepts on how children think and learn. Piaget gave us 4 stages of cognitive development. Each period in the development process is an advance over the previous one. To progress from one period to the next, children reorganize their thinking process to bring them closer to adult thinking.

Stage 1: The Sensorimotor Period (0-2 yrs.)

- 1-4 months- hand-mouth, eye-ear coordination (a rattle or tape of parent's voice).

- 4-8mos- learns to initiate, recognize and repeat to pleasurable experiences from environment - Memory traces - good game, peek a book

- 8-12 mos.- play activities to attain special goals - activities of own body separate fine activity of objects - experience separation anxiety - toys most played are colored boxes

- 12-18 mos.- capable of space and time perception as well as permanence - play throw and retrieve (like ball playing)

- 18-24 mos. – uses memory and imitation to act - play: blocks, colored plastic ring

Notes:
_____
_____
_____
_____

_____
_____
_____

Stage 2: Preoperational Thought (2-7 yrs.)

- Learns to use language and to represent objects by images and words

- Thinking is still egocentric: has difficulty taking the viewpoint of others

- Classifies objects by a single feature: e.g. groups together all the red blocks regardless of shape or all the square blocks regardless of color

Notes:
_____
_____
_____
_____
_____
_____
_____

Stage 3: Concrete Operations (7-11 yrs.)

- Can think logically about objects and events

- Achieves conservation of number (age 6), mass (age 7), and weight (age 9)

- Classifies objects according to several features and can order them in series along a single dimension such as size.

Notes:
_____
_____
_____
_____
_____
_____
_____

Stage 4: Formal Operations (11- adult)

- Can think logically about abstract propositions and test hypotheses systematically.

- Becomes concerned with the hypothetical, the future, and ideological problems.

Notes:
_____
_____
_____
_____
_____
_____
_____

Erik Erickson's Psychosocial Development (1902-1996)

One of the tenets of his theory is that a person's social view of self is more important than instinctual drives in determining the behavior, and allows for more optimistic view of the possibilities for human growth. Erickson offered 8 stages of psychosocial development covering the entire life span. At each stage, there is conflict between two opposing forces.

Stage 1: Trust vs. Mistrust (birth – 18 months)

- At this stage, an infant develops their sense of trust. With proper care and attention, the child will be able to trust. However, if this does not happen, it leads to mistrust in the child's life.

- Important events: Feeding and playing

Notes:
_____
_____
_____
_____
_____
_____
_____

Stage 2: Autonomy vs. Shame and Doubt (the toddler years, 18 months-3 years).

- Child is developing a sense of personal control over physical skills and a sense of independence.

- If not, they could start feeling ashamed and doubt their abilities, when caregivers are impatient and do everything for them.

- Important event: toilet training

Notes:
_____
_____
_____
_____
_____
_____
_____

Stage 3: Initiative vs. Guilt (Preschool ages 3-5 years old).

- Using initiative in planning or carrying out plans.

- Initiative has discovered that learning new things is fun.

- If not, they develop a sense of guilt over misbehavior regarding parent's limits or being criticized of activities done.

Notes:
_____
_____
_____
_____
_____
_____
_____

Stage 4: Industry vs. Inferiority (School ages 5-11 years of age).

- According to Erikson's model, the fourth stage of socioemotional development takes place from around six years of age to puberty. This stage is associated with mastering the developmental task of industry...

- Learn to follow the rules imposed by home and schools.

- If children are not instructed properly or felt to master or follow the developmental task of industry such as school rules, they can start believing they are inferior to others.

- Question: Am I competent?

Notes:

_____
_____
_____
_____
_____
_____
_____

Stage 5: Identity vs. Role Confusion (Adolescence ages 11-18 years old).

- Acquire a sense of identity. Who am I?

- The need to explore their independence and developing sense of self to fit in the society will emerge a strong sense of self.

- This stage is not mastered, the child can become confused about one role in life, once remain unsure of their beliefs and desires.

- Important events: Social Relationship such as making new friends

Notes:

_____
_____
_____
_____
_____
_____
_____

Stage 6: Intimacy vs. Isolation (Young adulthood, 18-40 years of age).

- Develop a relationship and joint identity with a partner.

- If healthy relationship and intimacy is not mastered, it can lead to isolation and stay away from meaningful relationships.

- Questions: if the person is ready for new relationships, or if there is a fear of rejection.

- Important events: The process of finding soul mate and building Romantic Relationship

Notes:

_____
_____
_____
_____
_____
_____
_____

Stage 7: Generativity vs. Stagnation (Middle adulthood, 40-65 years of age).

- Generativity is a concern for people besides self and family that usually develops during middle age; especially: a need to nurture and guide younger people and contribute to the next generation

- Making use of time and having a concern with helping others and guiding the next generation. "Making your Mark" on the world.

- Stagnation refers to failure to find way to contribute and finding fulfillment.

- Important events: Parenthood and Work

Notes:
_____
_____
_____
_____
_____
_____
_____

Stage 8: Integrity vs. Despair (Late adulthood 60-and up).

- Moment of reflecting back on life.

- Understand and accept the meaning of temporary life. Those feeling proud of their achievement will feel sense of integrity.

- In Despair, the adult may complain a lot about regrets, not having enough time, and not finding a meaning throughout life or life is wasted.

The Maslow, Piaget and Erickson's theories described in this chapter offer an overview of why we think, feel and act the way we do. You're encouraged to study these theories. They'll help you understand some of your needs and the needs of your clients. They more you understand your needs; the better you'll be in setting goals to fulfill them. You'll be able to seek specific help from God and from others.

Quiz:

1. Which of the following is not a fruit of the Spirit?

a. Kindness
b. Goodness
c. Faithfulness
d. Courage

2. According to Maslow's theory, which of the following need is required for our basic survival?

a. Food
b. Water
c. Sex
d. All of the above

3. According to our lecture, which of the following is not an example of security needs?

a. Health care
b. Safe neighborhoods
c. Shelter from the environment
d. Bank savings

4. True or False: All humans have a need to feel respected. This includes the need for self-esteem, self-respect and self-confidence

a. True
b. False

5. Which of the following statements is false?

a. The six basic needs can be categorized into the following: Spirit, Soul and Body.

b. Relationships such as friendships, romantic attachments and families help fulfill the need for companionship and acceptance.

c. Physiological needs are thought to be the most important and the most basic.

d. **Love and belonging** is the highest level of Maslow's hierarchy of needs.

Module 2: How problems are created

I believe that problems begin in the mind. They are interpretations of our reality. We all experience problems in life; however, we don't all respond to problems in the same way. The way you define your reality and expectations will make or break you.

How do you define your problems or reality? *"Problems are something that is difficult to deal with and understand; a source of trouble and worry; a feeling of not liking or wanting to do something" (Meriam-Webster Dictionary).* For me, problems are solutions yet to be uncovered. I believe as we change our mindset, we'll change our lives.

There are many reasons we have problems. As the authors of this manual, we want to be honest with you. We want you to know that we don't have all the answers. We only understand the mysteries of God in part as He reveals them to us. We don't know and understand all the reasons we experience pains and problems of life. In this manual, we only offer a simple view on why we face problems in life.

Notes:
_____
_____
_____
_____
_____
_____
_____

3 Basic reasons why we face problems in life:

1. Most problems are created in our minds.

We become whatsoever dominate our thinking on a consistent basis. *"For as he thinks in his heart, so is he [in behavior—one who manipulates]..." (Proverbs 23:7, AMP).* Our thinking determines our feelings; our feelings determine our actions; and our actions determine our results. Let's break this process down:

- Thoughts: Thoughts are the action or process of thinking. It's an idea, belief, story or opinion produced by events or occurring suddenly in the mind.

- Feelings: Feelings are emotional states or reactions of events and/or thoughts. It's the perception of events within the body related to our emotions. As human beings, we experience all kinds of emotions on a daily basis. New research suggests there are only four basic emotions: happy, sad, afraid/surprised, and angry/disgusted. We believe the more you understand your emotions, the more you can manage them and transform your life.

- Behaviors: Behaviors or actions are the way in which we act in response to a particular situation or stimulus. Our actions are the acts or process of doing something to achieve a goal or to get attention in order to satisfy a need. A behavior is both conditioned and determined by its own outcomes or consequences.

- Results: Results are things that happen as consequences of our actions. They're preceded as consequences of actions, circumstances and premises. If we want new results, we must change our mindset, our feelings and take actions to achieve the desired outcome.

Notes:

_____
_____
_____

_____
_____
_____
_____

2. We live in a sinful world.

We believe that one of the reasons we experience pain and problems in life is because we are not perfect; we make mistakes and live in a world with other imperfect people. Therefore, we are subject to the results of being in this world. We know that this is a simplified view of the world's problems and it cannot fully explain *all* problems. We believe that we have certain control and responsibility to care for what we can; the rest we leave up to God.

The truth is we are all subject to the problems of life. We all have different life stories and face different challenges. We are all dealt with different cards of life. For some, it is not the king, the queen or the ace. It is the unexpected children with a disability. For others, it is a broken home, blindness, the loss of a loved one or the cancer diagnosis at twenty-six-years-old. These are some of the issues people are dealing with. It does not matter if you are a Christian, a Jew, a Muslim or an atheist; we all have to face the reality of life. There is no easy way to play the cards we were dealt with by life.

When life gets difficult we recommend that you pray and seek help from those who are there to help you. Prayer will help you connect with God and reduce stress. We know that the less stressed we are, the more we are empowered to take actions toward our goals. Also, our minds will be clearer to face life's difficulties when there is less stress. Prayer itself will not eliminate our problems; living according to God's word is the other catalyst that releases God's power over our lives. As we pray and live a Godly life, we will be able to partner with God and use his power to overcome our troubles. The way we *handle* our problems determines our quality of life.

Notes:

_____
_____
_____
_____
_____
_____
_____

3. Our expectation is greater than the reality of life.

Have you ever stopped to think that we create our own problems by the simple strategy of wanting things to be different than how they actually are? We want other people to be different, especially our partners, children and friends! We want situations to be different instantly; we want ourselves to be different. The truth is, we can't be more than what we were created to be.

The desire to change what we cannot alter is a sure path to failure and unhappiness. It's like wanting the weather to be different. But the weather is what it is. We cannot change the weather, but we can accept it. We can choose to enjoy it however it is or we can complain about it and make ourselves feel miserable.

The other thing we never consider is that it is actually disrespectful to want to change things, especially others. In a subtle way, we are saying we know better than the other people. We imply that we know what's good for them; and this naturally creates a wall of resistance. In a relationship, it is like taking on the role of a parent and diminishing the other into the role of a child. Is it any wonder we get negative reactions from the other, even though we are convinced we are acting with the best intentions? And in fact, if we are really honest, our intentions are always in our *own* interest. If we really respected the other, we would accept them as they are, and we would dignify them by letting them decide how to live their own lives, even if it doesn't fit with our ideas. Even if they are on a path of self-destruction, it is *their* decision.

We cannot change people or certain things in life. We can only change our expectations and choose to accept what cannot be changed. We can give advice, but we cannot force people to take our counsel. Our clients and loved ones have the right to choose what is best for them. God created everyone with the right of free will.

The path to success and happiness is to accept what you cannot change; and do change what you can. If you want to be happy and achieve your goals, change whatsoever you can and surrender the rest to God. Besides, it's draining to focus on changing things or people that you cannot control.

The moral of the story is acceptance. Acceptance is a person's agreement to the reality. It's the process of recognizing a situation or condition—often a negative or uncomfortable situation without attempting to change it. For me, acceptance is not resignation; it is enjoying and celebrating, each other as the utterly unique and imperfect beings that we are. And that is the basis of much of my work. The serenity prayer is a great reminder for us to accept what we cannot change. *"Oh God, give us the serenity to accept what cannot be changed, the courage to change what can be changed, and the wisdom to know the one from the other"* (Elisabeth Sifton).

Notes:

_____
_____
_____
_____

Quiz:

1. According to Webster's Dictionary, what is the definition of problems?

   a. Something that is difficult to deal with and understand
   b. A source of trouble and worry
   c. A feeling of not liking or wanting to do something
   d. All of the above

2. Which is the correct pattern of problem development according to our lecture?

   a. Thinking → feelings → actions → results
   b. Thinking → actions → feelings → results
   c. Feelings → results → thinking → actions
   d. Results → actions → feelings → thinking

3. True or False – According to our lecture, prayer itself will eliminate our problems; living according to God's word is a weaker catalyst that releases God's power over our lives.

   a. True
   b. False

4. Which of the following statements are true?

   a. If we really respected others, we would accept them as they are.
   b. It does not matter if you are a Christian, a Jew, a Muslim or an atheist; we all have to face the reality of life.
   c. Behaviors or actions are the way in which we act in response to a particular situation or stimulus.
   d. All of the above.

5. True or False - We create our own problems by the simple strategy of wanting things to be how they actually are.

a. True
b. False

Module 3: How to help people in the process of healing and transformation.

"Therefore I urge you, brothers and sisters, by the mercies of God, to present your bodies [dedicating all of yourselves, set apart] as a living sacrifice, holy and well-pleasing to God, which is your rational (logical, intelligent) act of worship. And do not be conformed to this world [any longer with its superficial values and customs, but be [c]transformed and progressively changed [as you mature spiritually] by the renewing of your mind [focusing on godly values and ethical attitudes], so that you may prove [for yourselves] what the will of God is, that which is good and acceptable and perfect [in His plan and purpose for you]" (Romans 12:2, AMP).

Identify the fundamental need and the root cause of your clients' problems: "People have one basic personal need which requires two kinds of input for its satisfaction. The most basic need is a sense of personal worth…The two required inputs are significance… and security" (Lawrence Crabb, Effective Biblical Counseling). Your clients will present you with different symptoms, but the root cause of the problems will be the same: a loss of identity.

The counseling process serves to help the client redefine his or her identity in God; and that process is the foundation for healing and transformation. The use of any humanistic covering or fig leaves like Adam and Eve used to cover their shame and guilt from sin will not restore what we lost spiritually; only the love of Jesus can restore our identity and connection with God. *"Jesus answered, "I am the way and the truth and the life. No one comes to the Father except through me"* (John 14:6, NIV).

Notes:
_____
_____
_____

_____
_____
_____
_____

1. Repentance: "The process of change begins with honesty, which is a form of repentance. Repentance is an about-face movement from denial and rebellion to truth and surrender – from death to life... It is an internal shift in our perceived source of life" (Dan Allender, Wounded Heart). Repentance is simply taking responsibility for our actions that goes against the law of love and making a decision to surrender to the source: God.

Repentance vs. Penance: Repentance is what the Bible calls "Sorrow unto life." Penance, however, is referred to as "Sorrow unto death." Penance gives you an attitude of payback, whereas repentance leads you to plea for mercy. (2 Corinthians 7:10) The story of the prodigal son (Luke 15:11-32) demonstrates the difference between repentance and penance. The younger son became humbled and surrendered to his father's mercy, whereas the oldest son became angry and bitter. The acknowledgement of sin and wrongdoing can lead to one of the two. The counselor must pray and ask God to soften his or her client's heart toward repentance so the enemy doesn't take their hearts captive in the direction of penance.

Notes:

_____
_____
_____
_____
_____
_____
_____

2. Repentance, love and grace from God, yourself and others: The goal of repentance is to realize that we've messed up and we can't fix ourselves. Our only hope is to surrender ourselves to the grace and mercy of a loving God and humbly acknowledge our wickedness. That process opens the heart to receive God's love and forgiveness. If we open our hearts to God's love, mercy and grace, we'll be able to do the same for ourselves and others. However, if we refuse to repent and surrender, we will not be able to receive of God's love and thus won't be able to extend that same love to ourselves and others.

Notes:

_____
_____
_____
_____
_____
_____
_____

3. Transportation: Commit to the renewing of the mind through God's word: Change takes place when the current pain is greater than change itself (Romans 2:2). When we become tired of living apart from the healing grace of God, that's when we seek change. This change begins in our mindset. Mindset is a particular way of thinking: a focus, an attitude, a belief system or a set of opinions on something. The Bible urges us to renew our minds daily though the word of God. This renewal of the mind causes us to live according to God's Spirit and not the spirit of the world. Renewing our mind will help us "… *prove [for yourselves] what the will of God is, that which is good and acceptable and perfect [in His plan and purpose for you]" (Romans 12:2 AMP).* If we renew our mind, we'll get new thoughts. Our thoughts precede our actions; our actions form our habits; our habits create our character and our character produces our results.

Regardless of the desired result, change begins with the renewing of the mind.

Notes:
_____
_____
_____
_____
_____
_____
_____
_____
_____
_____

Reflections:

Since the fall of humanity, we all want to fulfill the void inside. We use all kinds of means to do so with no success. Some people abuse substances to fill their void. Others abuse sex to fulfill their needs, only to feel empty again and again. We try to fill a void that was created for God with earthly things. How have you tried to fill the void in your heart?

_____
_____
_____
_____
_____
_____
_____
_____
_____

Have you ever stopped to think that we create our own problems by the simple strategy of wanting things to be different, to how they actually are? How have you experienced this in your life?

_____
_____
_____
_____
_____
_____
_____
_____
_____

All humans have a need to feel respected. This includes the need for self-esteem, self-respect and self-confidence. Esteem encompasses the typical human desire to be accepted and valued by others. Satisfying this need and gaining acceptance and esteem helps people become more confident. Failing to gain recognition for accomplishments, however, can lead to feelings of failure or inferiority. How has this need affected your life?

_____
_____
_____
_____
_____
_____
_____
_____
_____

Our thinking determines our feelings; our feelings determine our actions; and our actions determine our results. What are your thoughts and feelings about this statement? Are you in agreement or disagreement? Explain why?

_____
_____
_____
_____
_____
_____
_____
_____
_____

Repentance is an about-face movement from denial and rebellion to truth and surrender—from death to life. It is an internal shift in our perceived source of life. What are your thoughts on this statement?

_____
_____
_____
_____
_____
_____
_____
_____

The job of the Christian counselor is to help the client find the spiritual repentance, healing and transformation in the Lord and allow that process to spill over to the soul, body and beyond. To help our clients live the abundant life that Jesus made available to all His children. "... *I came that they may have and enjoy life, and have it in abundance [to the full, till it overflows" (John 10:10, AMP).*

Chapter 4

How to Prepare Yourself to Successfully Start your Christian Counseling Ministry

"Study and do your best to present yourself to God approved, a workman [tested by trial] who has no reason to be ashamed, accurately handling and skillfully teaching the word of truth" (2 Timothy 2:15, AMP).

**Module 1: Develop in Character, Knowledge and skill
How do you develop in Character?**

1. How do you develop in character?

What is character? As you prepare for your counseling ministry, it's important to establish great character consistent to Christ like living. Character is what defines you. It's what people see in you. It's what people will say about you after you leave this earth. Your character is one of your most important possessions.

How to develop in character? The best way is keep your word and promises and take responsibility when you come short. "But let your 'Yes' be 'Yes,' and your 'No,' be 'No.' For whatever is more than these is from the evil one" (Matthew 5:37 & James 5:12).

Protect your **reputation**: "A good reputation and respect are worth much more than silver and gold" (Proverbs 22:1, CEV). As you allow the fruit of the Holy Spirit to develop in you, you will grow in character and maturity. As your character develops and solidifies, you will be able to make a tremendous impact in the lives of your clients.

Notes:

_____
_____
_____
_____
_____
_____
_____

How to develop in character as a counselor

Your thoughts precede your actions; your actions form your habits; your habits create your character and your character produces your destiny. Character development begins in your thoughts. If you change your thinking, you'll change your character. The Apostle Paul also gave this advice, "...Fix your thoughts on what is true and good and right. Think about things that are pure and lovely, and dwell on the fine, good things in others. Think about all you can praise God for and be glad about" (Philippians 4:8, TLB). Keeping your thoughts on such things will help you develop in character as a counselor.

Notes:

_____
_____
_____
_____
_____
_____
_____

2. What to do when you come short in your character development

No one is perfect. Everyone will miss the mark at some point in time. The best thing to do when you make a mistake is to admit it. It's okay if you don't have all knowledge needed to help everyone. I encourage you to be yourself and serve those you are called to care for the best you can. I ask that you reframe from being boastful and pretending that you understand all your clients' issues. I think it's reassuring to most of us to find out that we are all dealing with similar issues and that we aren't alone in the struggle of life. Be willing to be vulnerable about some of your struggles with your clients, it will help them see that they are not alone.

Notes:

_____
_____
_____
_____
_____
_____
_____

2. What kind of knowledge is required?

What do you need to know in order to effectively counsel people? As a successful counselor, it's imperative to commit to continued growth and development! *"The best counselors in the field aren't necessarily those who are most well known, but rather those who are always reaching toward greatness and flat out working harder than everyone else. These counselors are constantly questioning what they do and why, being brutally honest with themselves about their work and its outcomes. They are always soliciting feedback from their clients and colleagues, and seeking for the most frank assessments about what is working and what is not. Most of all, they are often so humble that they don't seek attention or the limelight, but just quietly go about their extraordinary commitment to helping others"* (Dr. Jeffrey A. Kottler).

Here is some important knowledge to develop are Christian counselor:

- Theology—Knowledge of the Bible and various scriptures dealing with how we ought to live as believers.

- Psychology—Knowledge on how people think, feel and act. Knowledge of human behavior and performance; individual differences in ability, personality, and interests; learning and motivation; psychological research methods and the assessment and treatment of behavioral and affective disorders or problems.

- Therapy and Counseling—Knowledge of principles, methods, and procedures for diagnosis, treatment, and rehabilitation of physical and mental dysfunctions, and for career counseling and guidance.

- Medicine—Knowledge of the information and techniques needed to diagnose and treat human injuries, diseases, and disorders. This includes symptoms, treatment alternatives, drug properties and interactions, and preventive healthcare measures.

- Customer and Personal Service—Knowledge of principles and processes for providing the best possible customer and personal care services. This includes customer needs assessment, meeting quality standards for services, and evaluating the satisfaction of your clients.

Notes:

_____
_____
_____
_____

_____
_____
_____

3. Essential Skills for a Developing Counselor?

Practice, practice, practice to develop your skills. Here's a list of important counseling skills:

LISTENING: Listening is the ability to accurately receive and interpret messages in the communication process. Listening is key to all effective communication, without the ability to listen effectively, messages are easily misunderstood. As a result, communication breaks down and the sender of the message can easily become frustrated or irritated. If there is one counseling skill you should aim to master, it is listening.

Notes:

_____
_____
_____
_____
_____
_____
_____

EMPATHY: "Empathy is the experience of understanding another person's condition from their perspective. You place yourself in their shoes and feel what they are feeling" (Psychologytoday.com) Empathy is a documented psychological phenomenon: If you see someone else get hurt, your own pain centers in the brain will light up. Scientists have demonstrated that you're more likely to help someone whose pain you feel. So, be empathetic to your clients, which in itself will go a long way in helping them heal.

Notes:

_____
_____
_____
_____
_____
_____
_____

ADVOCACY: Advocacy means to help or assist, and really that is the essence of counseling. Working with the client one-on-one isn't always enough. Making lasting differences in clients' lives often require challenging the prevailing environment and working to change it. There may be other underlying issues contributing to the presenting problem that the client will need your help with. In such cases, you may need to look for additional resources to help your clients address some of those contributing factors. As an advocate, you'll intercede on behalf of your clients and ensure that their human rights and needs are being addressed. You'll empower them to safely advocate for their needs and achieve their goals.

Notes:

_____
_____
_____
_____
_____
_____
_____

FLEXIBILITY: It's the ability and willingness to change. As a successful counselor, one of the skills to develop is your willingness to change by the leading of the Holy Spirit and for the best interest of your clients. The willingness to remain flexible as a counselor will expand your capacity to help your clients. It's important to have a plan and prepare for each counseling session, but be flexible for changes that may come up in the process.

Notes:
_____
_____
_____
_____
_____
_____
_____

Quiz:

1. Which of the following is not one of the essential skills for a developing counselor?

    a. Sympathy
    b. Listening
    c. Advocacy
    d. Flexibility

2. True/False: If you change your thinking, you'll change your character.

    a. True
    b. False

3. As you allow the fruit of the Holy Spirit to develop in you, you will:

    a. Grow in character
    b. Grow in maturity
    c. Grow in spirit
    d. All of the above

4. What is the best method to develop the essential skills of a developing counselor?

    a. Practice
    b. Study
    c. Prayer
    d. All of the above

5. True/False: Working with the client one-on-one is always enough.

    a. True
    b. False

Module 2: The Counseling Process

The counseling process is a continuous, cyclical series of interactions in which the counselor and client collaboratively set goals, formulate and implement action plans, and assess progress toward the goal(s). Throughout the process, new information is integrated, the counselor/client relationship is developed, and progress toward counseling goals is reassessed.

The counselor must develop an overall awareness of the entire counseling process across a number of interviews. We have broken the counseling process into five easy-to-follow steps. These steps represent a series of overall goals and expectations for the counselor as he/she progresses through a series of sessions with a client. If you follow these steps, they will help you get started in the right direction in your counseling ministry.

1. Assessment: The process by which counselors gather the information they need to form a holistic view of their clients and the problems with which they present. As a counselor, you will regularly assess your clients throughout the counseling process, especially in the early stages. Assessments are used as a basis for identifying problems, planning interventions, evaluating and/or diagnosing clients' needs, and informing clients and stakeholders. People are complex, and evaluations can provide the counselor with a broader and more accurate perspective of their clients. I recommend doing the following assessments at the beginning of the counseling process:

- Intake—The Initial Assessment: Intake interviews are the most common type of interview in counseling setting. They occur when a client first comes to seek help. The intake in counseling provides the counselor with information to understand clients, and may be therapeutic in clients' self understanding.

- Spiritual Development and Growth Assessment: A spiritual assessment will help you and your client identify their understanding of what it means to be a Christian, personal knowledge of Biblical truth, and their daily application of God's word in their lives.

- Bio-Psycho-Social Questionnaires: The bio-psycho-social assessment focuses on the biological, psychological, and social factors that play a significant role in human functioning in the context of disease or illness (George L. Engel, 1977).

Notes:

_____
_____
_____
_____
_____
_____
_____

2. Rapport Building: Proper rapport takes place when two or more people are in sync, or on the same thought vibration or wavelength because they feel similar and relate well to each other. Rapport is a term derived from the French word rapporteur (reporter), which means to bring back a message. It is the process of building trust and respect, characterized by a harmonious and mutual relationship. In building rapport, counselors demonstrate care, and strive to develop a trusting, collaborative relationship with their clients. When you develop rapport with your clients, they'll feel more comfortable to express themselves and will be more open to the counseling process. Here are three basic ways to build rapport:

- Practice Active Listening

- Be empathetic and show genuine concern

- Mirror your clients' body language, verbal and non-verbal clues. When you mirror your clients, you increase your likeability with them

Notes:

_____
_____
_____
_____
_____
_____
_____

3. Differential Diagnosis: Counselor tests hypotheses and develops an interaction between problem definition and information elicited from client. Counselor develops a case conceptualization as a helpful tool in the counseling process.

This will include a summary of the counselor's view of the problem, taking into consideration the common themes and what ties it all together. This is a synthesis of the above data collected that may illuminate the problem and guide the counseling plan. This format is continually revisited to some extent in each interview.

The diagnosis process may require a referral to other experts for further evaluations and tests in other to identify the appropriate diagnosis and recommendations. For example, if you are not an expert on depression and you have a client with symptoms related to this condition, we recommend that you refer your client to the best expert in that field.

Notes:

_____
_____

_____
_____
_____
_____
_____

4. Plan Development and implementation: Counselor helps client to set goals and behavioral objectives for behavior change. Counselor assists client in developing plan of action to resolve problem and reach objectives. Counselor develops a Counseling Plan in collaboration with the client. This will include a plan to be followed in the course of counseling to address the presenting problems and identified problems. This plan is consistent with the conceptualization of the problem and the theoretical orientation of the counselor.

Notes:

_____
_____
_____
_____
_____
_____
_____

5. Termination: Termination occurs when the goals that are mutually agreed upon between the counselor and the client have been achieved, or the problem for which a client has entered into counseling has become more manageable or is resolved. Termination is the final stage of the counseling process, but is not something that should be broached during your last (or next to last) session with a client. Doing so does not allow for the proper amount of time for counselor and client to process what termination means, how the client will handle the conclusion of the counseling relationship, and what follow-up contact or transitioning needs to happen for the client.

Termination should be among the first topics that you and your client discuss. This process should be clearly articulates with the client, especially if it's a first-time client. "The therapist must be clear from the first contact, unless there are mitigating circumstances that the intent of treatment is to help the client function without the therapist" (Steven Aaron Kramer, 1990).

As a counselor, you are ethically bound to communicate to your client how long you will be available to counsel them, to discuss openly the timeline of your relationship, and to make appropriate referrals or recommendations at the conclusion of your relationship. Here are some helpful guidelines for effectively moving your clients toward termination:

- Remind clients of the approaching ending of the sessions with you. This should be done at least two to three sessions prior to the final one. This provides you an opportunity to ask clients to talk about relationships that have ended in their past, how they have ended, and how that might affect the end of this counseling relationship. You can also ask clients what they would like to focus on during their remaining time with you.

- Allow clients to talk about their feelings surrounding termination. They will likely have many emotions to work through, and time should be spent acknowledging and processing them. Be aware of your own feelings surrounding the termination process. Acknowledge your feelings, your ambivalence about termination, etc. If you are good at what you do, people will not need to continue to see you for help. They will have the tools to help themselves.

- Review the tools and skills that clients have acquired through the counseling process. These tools will be critical in helping clients be self-sufficient in handling problems that might have previously brought them to counseling. If there are additional resources that you feel your client would benefit from for continued personal growth, make appropriate referrals and make your client aware of them.

- If possible, have an open-door policy. Once termination has ended, clients may want to return a few months or years later to refocus or to "check-in." This is often impossible in the training setting, but something to keep in mind for your professional career.

Notes:
_____
_____
_____
_____
_____
_____
_____

Quiz:

1. Which of the following occurs throughout the counseling process?

   a. New information is integrated
   b. The counselor/client relationship is developed
   c. Progress toward counseling goals is reassessed
   d. All of the above

2. A spiritual assessment will help you and your clients identify their understanding of which of the following?

   a. What it means to be a Christian, personal knowledge of Biblical truth, and their daily application of God's word in their lives.
   b. The core message of their church's denomination.
   c. The theological definition of the Trinity.
   d. None of the above

3. Which of the following is not one of the three basic ways to build rapport?

   a. Be empathetic and show genuine concern
   b. Mirror your clients' body language, verbal and non-verbal clues. (When you mirror your clients, you increase your likeability with them.)
   c. Practice Active Listening
   d. Pray at the beginning of each session

4. True/False: Termination should be one of the last topics that you and your client discuss.

   a. True
   b. False

5. As a counselor, which of the following are you ethically bound to communicate to your client?

a. How long you will be available to counsel them.
b. Discuss openly the timeline of your relationship
c. Make appropriate referrals or recommendations at the conclusion of your relationship
d. All of the above

Module 3: 5 Tips to Successfully Start your Christian Counseling Ministry

It's not enough to know that you are called into counseling ministry. If you want to respond to the call to become a counselor and to change lives, you must take action. Action is what separates those who are in the team and those who are watching the game. However, in order to take action you will need to know what to do. In this section, I will give you five practical tips you can use to launch your Christian counseling ministry. They are as follows:

1. Clearly define your vision of your counseling ministry. Write it in plain English. Make it simple for you and others to remember. Creating a strong vision is one of the most important steps in starting anything. A vision statement compels people to do something, change something and become something. It is this drive that can transform a ministry into a strong, vibrant, rewarding opportunity for everyone who comes into contact with it.

Notes:
_____
_____
_____
_____
_____
_____
_____

2. Develop a S.M.A.R.T. plan for your ministry. A plan that establishes goals and objectives as well as steps for achieving them is at the heart of a successful counseling ministry. Time spent on developing an effective plan will pay dividends later because it will provide a framework for guiding your efforts. Developing a plan involves creating an

effective planning environment, formulating the plan, and developing administrative support for the plan.

S – Specific Goals
M – Measurable
A – Attainable
R – Relevant
T – Time-Bound

Notes:
_____
_____
_____
_____
_____
_____
_____

3. Develop a team: Success is a team sport. Enlist the help of others to help you start your ministry. Get a mentor or a coach in your team. Get someone who is successful doing the type of ministry you want to start and volunteer with them. There is no point in reinventing the wheel. Learn from others who are already in ministry. Pray and ask the Lord to lead you to the right mentor or coach to help lead and guide you in the process. Whatever you do, just don't do it alone—enlist the help of others.

Notes:
_____
_____
_____
_____
_____
_____
_____

4. Spread the word: Make a list of friends, family members and church members and let them know that you've started a Christian counseling ministry. They may refer people to you who need your services. Here are three ways you can spread the word:

- Start a FREE blog or a website and drive traffic to it
- Use social media and other online marketing sites to promote your ministry.
- Advertise in your ministry in your church bulletin and local events.

Notes:

_____
_____
_____
_____
_____
_____
_____

5. Commit to growth and development as a counselor: As you continue to take action toward your call, God will open new doors for you to serve. Commit to develop your character, skills and knowledge as a counselor; and to improve your counseling style and process. Our prayer is that the Lord will use you to fulfill his purpose for your life and the lives of others.

Notes:

_____
_____
_____
_____
_____
_____
_____
_____

Reflections:

Earlier in this chapter we talked about character development and its value in your counseling ministry. We recommended that you become willing to be vulnerable about some of your struggles with your clients, as that will help them see that they are not alone. In reflecting on this section, write about one character flaw that you need God's help with. Tell God how you feel about this issue and how you need his help.

_____
_____
_____
_____
_____
_____
_____
_____

Listening is the ability to accurately receive and interpret messages in the communication process. Listening is key to all effective communication, without the ability to listen effectively messages are easily misunderstood. As a result, communication breaks down and the sender of the message can easily become frustrated or irritated. If there is one counseling skill you should aim to master, it is listening. How would you grade your listening skills? How are you going to improve your listening skills?

_____
_____
_____
_____
_____
_____
_____
_____

Proper rapport takes place when two or more people are in sync, or on the same thought vibration or wavelength because they feel similar and relate well to each other. How do you currently build rapport with people? Is this a strong area for you, or is it a challenging area?

_____
_____
_____
_____
_____
_____
_____
_____

In module two we talked about the termination process. We recommended that you allow clients to talk about their feelings surrounding termination because they will likely have many emotions to work through, and time should be spent acknowledging and processing them. This will provide you an opportunity to ask clients to talk about relationships that have ended in their past and how they have dealt with them. How have relationships ended in your past, and how have you dealt with such issues?

_____
_____
_____
_____
_____
_____
_____
_____

Develop a team: Success is a team sport. Enlist the help of others to help you start your ministry. Get a mentor or a coach on your team. Get someone who is successful doing the type of ministry you want to start, and volunteer with them. There is no point in reinventing the wheel. Learn from others who are already in ministry. Pray and ask the Lord to lead you to the right mentor or coach to help lead and guide you in the process. Whatever you do, just don't do it alone—enlist the help of others. How do you feel about having a mentor or a coach? Do you feel that having a mentor will help your ministry, or restrict it?

_____
_____
_____
_____
_____
_____
_____
_____

Conclusion

This counseling course is an introduction to Biblical-based class with special attention given to tough issues that distress today's generation. The ultimate goal was to introduce you to the Biblical answers for modern-day problems. We hope this course provided you an overview of basic resources and knowledge that apply to a broad scope of issues you'll face in your counseling ministry.

Upon successful completion of this course, you'll be able to:

- Understand why the Bible is the Ultimate Authority and Guide for Christian Counseling

- Understand the Role of the Holy Spirit in Christian Counseling

- Understand the Process of Repentance, Healing and Transformation

- Learn How to Prepare Yourself to Successfully Start your Christian Counseling Ministry

To learn more about this course and other programs by James Justin and Dr. Lauretta Justin, visit CoachJamesJustin.com!

We leave you with this prayer …

God, help me to share my client's (or friend's) pain without letting her pain overwhelm me.

Help me to feel their hurt without feeling consumed by it.

Help me to enter their chaos without being sucked into it.

Help me to approach their problems without feeling the need to fix them.

Help me share their grief without trying to rescue them from it.

Help me to bear witness to their past without feeling the weight of its devastation.

Help me to celebrate their growth without taking credit for it.

Help me to hear of abuse without turning cynical; broken relationships without becoming bitter; neglectful parenting without being judgmental.

Help me to hold hope for others even when I'm struggling to hold hope for myself.

Help me to keep my heart open even after it breaks.

And help me to draw closer to your heart every time I'm overwhelmed by the pain in mine. Amen!

This prayer is quoted from this site: (revivingidentity.wordpress.com/2011/04/13/a-counselors-prayer).

References

Spiritual Health

The Holy Bible. New King James Version (NKJV). (1982). Nashville, TN: Thomas Nelson, Inc.

Warren, R. (2002). PURPOSE DRIVEN LIFE: WHAT ON EARTH AM I HERE FOR? Grand Rapids, Michigan: Zondervan.

McGee, R.S. (2003). THE SEARCH FOR SIGNIFICANCE: SEEING YOUR TRUE WORTH THROUGH GOD'S EYES. Nashville, TN: Thomas Nelson.

Lewis, C.S (1960). THE FOUR LOVES. London, England: Geoffrey Bles.

Freed, P.D. (2006). MIGHTY MEN OF GOD. Orlando, FL: Insight Publishing.

Eldredge, J. & Eldredge, S. (2011). CAPTIVATING REVISED & UPDATED: UNVEILING THE MYSTERY OF A WOMAN'S SOUL. Nashville, TN: Thomas Nelson, Inc.

Eldredge, J. (2011). WILD AT HEART REVISED & UPDATED: DISCOVERING THE SECRET OF A MAN'S SOUL. Nashville, TN: Thomas Nelson, Inc.

Jakes, T.D. (1998). REPOSITION YOURSELF: LIVING LIFE WITHOUT LIMITS. Atria Books: New York City, NY.

Psychological Health

Dweck, C. (2007). MINDSET: THE NEW PSYCHOLOGY OF SUCCESS. ISBN-13: 978-0345472328. Ballantine Books: New York City, New York.

Maltz, M (1989). PSYCHO-CYBERNETICS, A NEW WAY TO GET MORE LIVING OUT OF LIFE. Chicago, IL: Pocket Books.

Coué, É (2011). SELF-MASTERY THROUGH CONSCIOUS AUTOSUGGESTION. Space Independent Publishing Platform: Mustang, OK.

William, W. A. (2010). THOUGHT VIBRATION, OR, THE LAW OF ATTRACTION IN THE THOUGHT WORLD. Qontro Legacy: Clinton, MA.

Schwartz, D.J. (1987). THE MAGIC OF THINKING BIG. Chicago, IL: Touchstone.

Rosenberg, M. (1965). SOCIETY AND THE ADOLESCENT SELF-IMAGE. Princeton, NJ: Princeton University Press.

Branden, N. (2001). THE PSYCHOLOGY OF SELF-ESTEEM: A REVOLUTIONARY APPROACH TO SELF-UNDERSTANDING THAT LAUNCHED A NEW ERA IN MODERN PSYCHOLOGY. New York City, NY: Jossey-Bass.

Stoop, D. (2003). YOU ARE WHAT YOU THINK. Ada, MI: Revell Publishing.

Cloud, H & Townsend, J. (2002). BOUNDARIES: WHEN TO SAY YES, HOW TO SAY NO TO TAKE CONTROL OF YOUR LIFE. Grand Rapids, Michigan: Zondervan.

Meyer, J. (2005). BATTLEFIELD OF THE MIND DEVOTIONAL: 100 INSIGHTS THAT WILL CHANGE THE WAY YOU THINK. Faithwords: Nashville, Tennessee.

Meyer, J. (2011). LIVING BEYOND YOUR FEELINGS: CONTROLLING EMOTIONS SO THEY DON'T CONTROL YOU. Faithwords: Nashville, Tennessee.

Meyer, J. (2012). POWER THOUGHTS: 12 STRATEGIES TO WIN THE BATTLE OF THE MIND. Faithwords: Nashville, Tennessee.

Anderson, N.T. & Miller, R. (1999). Freedom from Fear: Overcoming Worry and Anxiety. Harvest House Publishers: Eugene, Oregon.

Cloud, H. & Townsend, J. (2000). BOUNDARIES IN DATING. Grand Rapids, Michigan: Zondervan.

Ziglar, Z. & Ziglar, T. (2012). BORN TO WIN: FIND YOUR SUCCESS CODE. Dallas, TX, Success Books.

Bailey, S.T. (2007). RELEASE YOUR BRILLIANCE: THE 4 STEPS TO TRANSFORMING YOUR LIFE AND REVEALING YOUR GENIUS TO THE WORLD. New York City, NY: HarperCollins Publishers.

Johnson, S and Blanchard, K. (1998). WHO MOVED MY CHEESE? AN AMAZING WAY TO DEAL WITH CHANGE IN YOUR WORK AND IN YOUR LIFE. New York City, NY: Publisher: G. P. Putnam's Sons.

Physical Health

Oz, M.C. & Roizen, M.F. (2005). YOU: THE OWNER'S MANUAL, UPDATED AND EXPANDED EDITION: AN INSIDER'S GUIDE TO THE BODY THAT WILL MAKE YOU HEALTHIER AND YOUNGER. ISBN-13: 978-0060765316. Collins: New York, NY.

Colbert, D. (2006). The Seven Pillars of Health: The Natural Way to Better Health for Life. ISBN-13: 978-1591858157. Siloam: Lake Mary, Fla.

Davis, A. (1975). YOU CAN GET WELL. ISBN-13: 978-0879040338. Benedict Lust Pubns: East Wenatchee, WA.

Davis, A. (1954). LET'S EAT RIGHT TO KEEP FIT. Harcourt Brace Publishers, San Diego, California.

Trudeau, K. (2004). NATURAL CURES THEY DON'T WANT YOU TO KNOW ABOUT. Alliance Publishing Group: Birmingham, AL.

Campbell, A. (2009). THE WOMEN'S HEALTH BIG BOOK OF EXERCISES: FOUR WEEKS TO A LEANER, SEXIER, HEALTHIER YOU! Rodale Books: Emmaus, PA.

Phillips, B. (1999). BODY FOR LIFE: 12 WEEKS TO MENTAL AND PHYSICAL STRENGTH. William Morrow: New York City, NY.

Rogers, S. A. (2000). NO MORE HEARTBURN: STOP THE PAIN IN 30 DAYS--NATURALLY: THE SAFE, EFFECTIVE WAY TO PREVENT AND HEAL CHRONIC GASTROINTESTINAL DISORDERS. Kensington Books: New York City, NY.

Healthy Relationship

Justin, J. (2016). 7 STEPS TO DEVELOP HEALTHY RELATIONSHIPS WITH ANYONE. Orlando, FL: CoachJamesJustin.com.

Carnegie, D. (2009). HOW TO WIN FRIENDS AND INFLUENCE PEOPLE. New York, NY: Simon & Schuster, Inc.

Whelchel, L. (2010). FRIENDSHIP FOR GROWN-UPS: WHAT I MISSED AND LEARNED ALONG THE WAY. Nashville, TN: Thomas Nelson, Inc.

McGinnis, A.L. (2004). THE FRIENDSHIP FACTOR: HOW TO GET CLOSER TO THE PEOPLE YOU CARE FOR. Minneapolis, MN: Augsburg Fortress Publishers.

Sanders, T. (2006). THE LIKEABILITY FACTOR: HOW TO BOOST YOUR L-FACTOR AND ACHIEVE YOUR LIFE'S DREAMS. New York City, NY: Three Rivers Press.

Fine, D. (2005) THE FINE ART OF SMALL TALK: HOW TO START A CONVERSATION, KEEP IT GOING, BUILD NETWORKING SKILLS -- AND LEAVE A POSITIVE IMPRESSION. New York City, NY: Hyperion.

Wood, Julia (2001). COMMUNICATION MOSAIC: AN INTRODUCTION TO THE FIELD OF COMMUNICATION. Belmont, California: Wadsworth Publishing.

Mehrabian, A. (2nd Ed.). (1981). SILENT MESSAGES: IMPLICIT COMMUNICATION OF EMOTIONS AND ATTITUDES. Belmont, CA: Wadsworth. ISBN 0-534-00910-7.

Mehrabian, A. (1972). NONVERBAL COMMUNICATION. Chicago, IL: Aldine-Atherton. ISBN 0-202-30966-5.

Arterburn, S. & Rinck, M.J. (2003). FINDING MR. RIGHT: AND HOW TO KNOW WHEN YOU HAVE. Nashville, TN: Thomas Nelson, Inc.

Page, S. (2002). IF I'M SO WONDERFUL, WHY AM I STILL SINGLE? TEN STRATEGIES THAT WILL CHANGE YOUR LOVE LIFE FOREVER. New York City, NY: Three Rivers Press.

Arterburn, S. & Stoeker, F. (2009). EVERY MAN'S BATTLE. New York City, NY: Three Rivers Press.

Ethridge, S. & Arterburn, S. (2009). EVERY WOMAN'S BATTLE. New York City, NY: Three Rivers Press.

Gray, J. (2004). MEN ARE FROM MARS, WOMEN ARE FROM VENUS: THE CLASSIC GUIDE TO UNDERSTANDING THE OPPOSITE SEX. New York, NY: Harper Paperbacks.

Toth, J. K. DRIVING THE NAIL HOME.

Freed, P.D. & Freed, S. (2001). THE MARRIAGE MAKERS. Orlando, FL: Insight Publishing.

Wheat, E. & Wheat, G. (2010). INTENDED FOR PLEASURE: SEX TECHNIQUE AND SEXUAL FULFILLMENT IN CHRISTIAN MARRIAGE. Ada, MI: Baker Publishing Group.

Meier, R. Meier, P. & Minirth, F. (1997). SEX IN THE CHRISTIAN MARRIAGE. Ada, MI: Fleming H. Revell Company.

Whitehead, B.D. (1998). THE DIVORCE CULTURE: RETHINKING OUR COMMITMENTS TO MARRIAGE AND FAMILY. New York City, NY: Vintage.

Chapman, G.D. (2009). THE 5 LOVE LANGUAGES: THE SECRET TO LOVE THAT LASTS. Chicago: IL: Northfield Publishing.

Gottman, J. M. & Silver, N. (2000). THE SEVEN PRINCIPLES FOR MAKING MARRIAGE WORK: A PRACTICAL GUIDE FROM THE COUNTRY'S FOREMOST RELATIONSHIP EXPER. London, England: Orion Paperbacks.

Keller, T. & Keller, K. (2011). THE MEANING OF MARRIAGE: FACING THE COMPLEXITIES OF COMMITMENT WITH THE WISDOM OF GOD. New York City, NY: Dutton Adult.

Omartian, S. (2007). THE POWER OF A PRAYING WIFE. Eugene, OR: Publisher: Harvest House Publishers.

Rosberg, G. & Rosberg, B. (2002). BULLET-PROOF YOUR MARRIAGE: 6 SECRETS TO A FOREVER MARRIAGE. Carol Stream, IL: Tyndale House Publishers.

Gregoire, S.W. (2012). 31 DAYS TO GREAT SEX. New York City, NY: Smashwords.

Financial Health

Justin, J. (2016). 12 TIPS TO FINANCIAL FREEDOM: THE SIMPLY GUIDE TO SUCCESSFULLY MANAGE YOUR PERSONAL FINANCE. Orlando, FL: CoachJamesJustin.com.

Hill, N. (1928). THE LAW OF SUCCESS. New York City, NY: Tribeca Books.

Hill, N (1937). THINK AND GROW RICH. Ralston, Nebraska: The Ralston Society.

Wattles, W.D. (1910). THE SCIENCE OF GETTING RICH. Elizabeth Towne Company: Holyoke, MA.

Hill, N. (2009). HOW TO SELL YOUR WAY THROUGH LIFE. Street Hoboken, NJ: Wiley.

Tracy, B. (2006). THE PSYCHOLOGY OF SELLING: INCREASE YOUR SALES FASTER AND EASIER THAN

YOU EVER THOUGHT POSSIBLE. Nashville, TN: Thomas Nelson.

Qubein, N. (2006). CLOSE LIKE A PRO: SELLING STRATEGIES FOR SUCCESS UNABRIDGED AUDIOBOOK. ISBN–13: 978-1596590755. Your Coach Digital: www.amazon.com.

Port, M. (2010). BOOK YOURSELF SOLID: THE FASTEST, EASIEST, AND MOST RELIABLE SYSTEM FOR GETTING MORE CLIENTS THAN YOU CAN HANDLE EVEN IF YOU HATE MARKETING AND SELLING. Hoboken, NJ: Wiley-Blackwell Publishing.

Ramsey, D. (3rd Edition). (2009). THE TOTAL MONEY MAKEOVER: A PROVEN PLAN FOR FINANCIAL FITNESS. Nashville, TN: Thomas Nelson, Inc.

Burchard, B. (2011). THE MILLIONAIRE MESSENGER. Free Press Publishing.

Orman, S. (2006). THE 9 STEPS TO FINANCIAL FREEDOM: PRACTICAL AND SPIRITUAL STEPS SO YOU CAN STOP WORRYING. Three Rivers Press.

Kiyosaki, K. (2006). RICH WOMAN: A BOOK ON INVESTING FOR WOMEN: BECAUSE I HATE BEING TOLD WHAT TO DO! Rich Press: Gladewater, Texas.

Kiyosaki, R.T. (2011). RICH DAD'S CASHFLOW QUADRANT: RICH DAD'S GUIDE TO FINANCIAL FREEDOM. Scottsdale, AZ.: Plata Publishing.

Fridson, M.S. (2001). HOW TO BE A BILLIONAIRE: PROVEN STRATEGIES FROM THE TITANS OF WEALTH. Wiley, John & Sons, Inc.

Bartmann, B. (2006). BILLIONAIRE: SECRETS TO SUCCESS. Executive Books.

Dean, T. (2006). FINANCIAL FREEDOM: A STEP-BY-STEP PRACTICAL GUIDE FOR WALKING IN GOD'S BLESSINGS. Dunnellon, FL: mymarketingcoach, LLC.

About the Authors

Pastor James Justin

A born leader, James Justin hasn't let any obstacles stand in his way. And he has the skills to make sure your obstacles are broken and no longer stand in *your* way.

"It's my passion to inspire and to help you transform your life to greater success, joy and happiness! This passion led me to earn my master's degree in the field of counseling and dedicate my life to speaking, coaching and helping people like you for over 20 years!"

James Justin is an entrepreneur, pastor, speaker, author and life coach. He earned his Master of Social Work (MSW) degree from Boston College, and his Bachelor of Social Work (BSW) degree from Eastern Nazarene College in Quincy, Massachusetts.

James worked as a Professional Counselor for the State of Florida for 7+ years prior to pursuing his passion and his dream: to help and make an impact in the private sector.
In 2011, James and his wife, Dr. Lauretta, co-authored and published their first book "Express Yourself," and in 2013 James published his solo book project titled "How to Develop Meaningful Relationships!"

James is committed to helping create transformational growth with each and every one of his clients.
James and Lauretta are the proud parents of three incredible and very active boys: Nathan, Sean and Joshua. They spend the majority of their free time focusing on "the boys!"

To contact James, visit coachjamesjustin.com!

Dr. Lauretta Justin

Dr. Lauretta is an entrepreneur, eye doctor, speaker, author and singer! She is the co-author of the 2011 book "Express Yourself!" In 2015, she released her debut Christmas music album titled, "The Spirit of Christmas!"

She is the founder and president of Millennium Eye Center, where she practices optometry. She is licensed and board certified to practice optometry in the state of Florida. She earned her Doctor of Optometry (O.D.) degree from the prestigious New England College of Optometry, with clinical honors. She completed her Bachelor of Science degree in Biology at Montclair State University in Montclair, New Jersey. Lauretta is listed in the 2011 edition of the Heritage Registry of Who's Who, and is a proud member of the American Optometry Association, the Florida Optometry Association, the Central Florida Society of Optometric Physicians, and Vision Source.

To contact Dr. Lauretta, visit DrLaurettaJustin.com!

www.ingramcontent.com/pod-product-compliance
Lightning Source LLC
LaVergne TN
LVHW061312060426
835507LV00019B/2111